In Their Fathers' Footsteps

The Story of the
James Donaldson Group

Another load leaving the Wemyss yard in Leven under the watchful eye of manager Jim Cuthbert in the early 1960s.

In Their Fathers' Footsteps

The Story of the
James Donaldson Group

NIGEL WATSON

Published 2021 by

St Matthew's Press

10 St Matthew's Terrace

Leyburn

North Yorkshire DL8 5EL

ISBN 978-1-8383994-5-0

Design and artwork by Matthew Wilson:
Editorial + Publishing Design/www.mexington.com

Printed and bound by Pureprint Group,
Bellbrook Park, Uckfield, West Sussex TN22 1PL

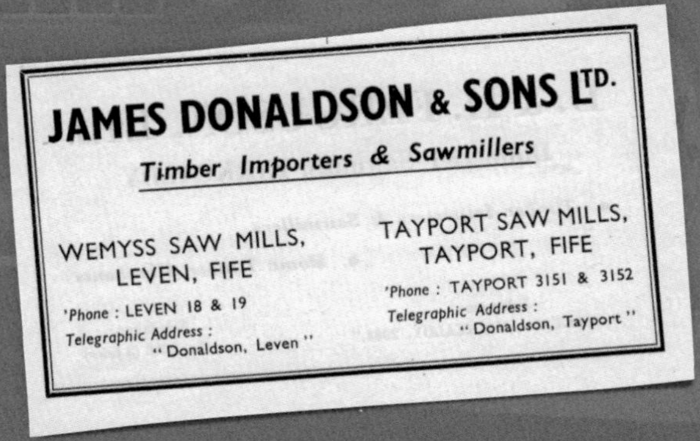

JAMES DONALDSON & SONS L^{TD.}

Timber Importers & Sawmillers

WEMYSS SAW MILLS,
LEVEN, FIFE

'Phone : LEVEN 18 & 19

Telegraphic Address :
" Donaldson, Leven "

TAYPORT SAW MILLS,
TAYPORT, FIFE

'Phone : TAYPORT 3151 & 3152

Telegraphic Address :
" Donaldson, Tayport "

Contents

Simplified Family Tree

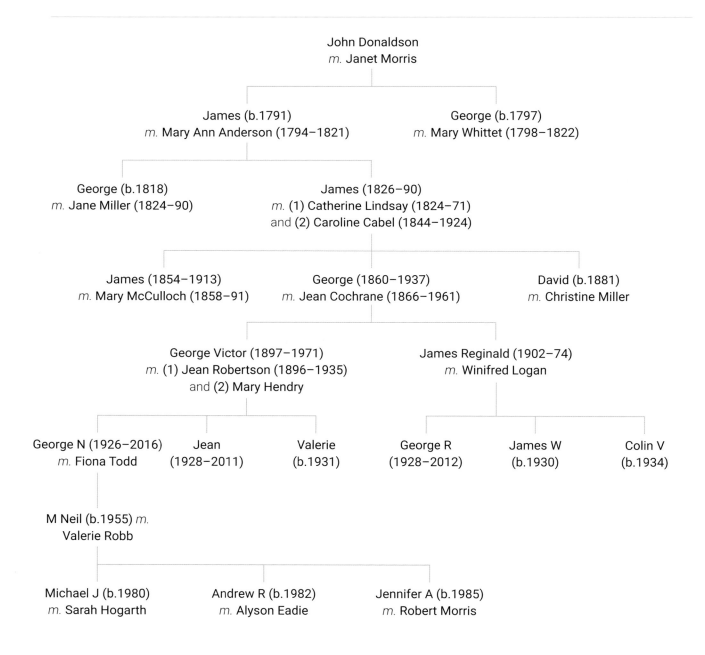

John Donaldson
m. Janet Morris

James (b.1791)
m. Mary Ann Anderson (1794–1821)

George (b.1797)
m. Mary Whittet (1798–1822)

George (b.1818)
m. Jane Miller (1824–90)

James (1826–90)
m. (1) Catherine Lindsay (1824–71)
and (2) Caroline Cabel (1844–1924)

James (1854–1913)
m. Mary McCulloch (1858–91)

George (1860–1937)
m. Jean Cochrane (1866–1961)

David (b.1881)
m. Christine Miller

George Victor (1897–1971)
m. (1) Jean Robertson (1896–1935)
and (2) Mary Hendry

James Reginald (1902–74)
m. Winifred Logan

George N (1926–2016)
m. Fiona Todd

Jean
(1928–2011)

Valerie
(b.1931)

George R
(1928–2012)

James W
(b.1930)

Colin V
(b.1934)

M Neil (b.1955) *m.*
Valerie Robb

Michael J (b.1980)
m. Sarah Hogarth

Andrew R (b.1982)
m. Alyson Eadie

Jennifer A (b.1985)
m. Robert Morris

Foreword

I have spent my whole adult life working for James Donaldson & Sons Ltd (JDS) and now at the age of 65 it is time for me to take more of a back seat. I do that safe in the knowledge that the next generation are firmly in control and they will put their stamp on the company in the years ahead.

I have enjoyed my time in the timber trade and would do it all again if I could. This amazing trade is made by the people that congregate towards it. They are good people, dedicated people, kind people and honest people – a bit like a family company, really.

When I joined the company in 1975 there must have been 30 or 40 other members of the Scottish Timber Industry Association. Many were household names and I was fortunate enough to work with them all. Sadly, barring two that I am aware of, the others have all gone. Liquidations, winding down and takeovers have seen them all confined to history. How lucky we are not just to have survived, but now to be one of the pre-eminent timber companies in both Scotland and the UK.

JDS is unique. For a family company to survive three generations is unusual; for that same company to now be run by the sixth generation is extraordinary. Those similar traits to the timber trade of good, dedicated, kind and honest people are all to be found in abundance at JDS but there is more: loyalty, vision, values, culture, professionalism and a deep sense of belonging and of wanting to be the best.

In my time in working with the company I have been privileged and honoured to work with the best people in the industry. It has been very challenging at times, but it has also been fun and hugely rewarding.

This book explores not only the history of a whole trade but also the history of a family and the friends and colleagues who support it. I hope you enjoy the read.

Neil Donaldson
Honorary President

*James Donaldson (1826–1890),
founder of James Donaldson & Sons.*

'Every Description of Baltic and American Timber'

The early years of James Donaldson & Sons 1860–89

1

I n October 1888, the *Timber Trades Journal* published a Scottish supplement to accompany its main edition, testifying to the prosperous state of the timber industry north of the border. There was a lengthy list of Scottish timber-importing ports, including Aberdeen, Alloa, Borrowstounness, Dundee, Fraserburgh, Glasgow, Grangemouth, Granton, Greenock, Inverness, Kirkcaldy, Leith, Lerwick, Montrose and Wick. The supplement was filled with advertisements from timber merchants, importers and brokers. One firm boasted that it carried 'Every Description of Baltic and American Timber' and had recently added Quebec timber to its stocks.

That firm was James Donaldson & Sons, timber merchants of Tayport, on the opposite bank of the River Tay from the busy industrial port of Dundee. In the three decades since the founding of the firm, James Donaldson had become a respected figure in the Scottish trade and was often invited to act as an arbitrator in disputes. He enjoyed just as much respect locally and acted as a justice of the peace for the County of Fife. His eldest son, James junior, was a magistrate for the newly constituted burgh of Tayport, coming top of the poll. He became a partner in the firm alongside his father in 1876 and was joined by his younger brother, George, in 1888.

The timber trade was a completely new venture for the Donaldson family. Previous generations of Donaldsons had been skilled artisans. The first link with timber comes with James's grandfather, John Donaldson, who lived at Dalreitchmoor in the parish of Kilspindie, eight miles from Perth, where he earned his living as a wright and a hand-loom weaver.

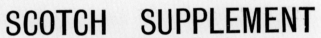

SCOTCH SUPPLEMENT
To the Timber Trades Journal.   OCTOBER 27, 1888

ANIMAL VEGETABLE MINERAL FISH

OILS
JUTE WOOL CLOTH
CYLINDER ENGINE MACHINERY

MacARTHUR & JACKSON, OIL MANUFACTURERS, GLASGOW.
Agents wanted where not already represented.

Taylor's BELT Patent FASTENER
DAVID S. BRYSON,
Trades Lane, DUNDEE.

SINGLETON, DUNN, & CO.,
TIMBER BROKERS,
27, UNION STREET, GLASGOW.
Telegram Address—
"SINGLETONS, GLASGOW."

ALLISON, COUSLAND, & CO.,
Timber, Ship, & Insurance Brokers,
154, St. Vincent Street,
GLASGOW.

JAMES KENNEDY & CO.
Home & Foreign Timber Merchants,
69, BUCHANAN STREET
GLASGOW.
Telegraphic Address—
"LIGNUM" GLASGOW.

EDMISTON & MITCHELLS,
TIMBER BROKERS,
33, Renfield Street, GLASGOW.
Telegraphic Address—
"EDMISTON," GLASGOW.

WRIGHT & BREAKENRIDGE,
TIMBER BROKERS,
69, St. George's Place, Glasgow.
Telegraphic Address "BRAKRILGR."

Robert Hamilton & Co.,
TIMBER BROKERS,
75, ST. GEORGE'S PLACE,
Glasgow,
Telegraphic Address—" WALNUT, GLASGOW."

THOMSON & GRAY,
TEAK IMPORTERS,
40, WEST NILE STREET,
GLASGOW.
Telegraphic Address—"TEAK," GLASGOW.

CHAS. JAMES KERR,
TIMBER BROKER,
40, WEST NILE ST.,
GLASGOW.

MALCOLM CARSWELL & CO.
TIMBER BROKERS,
11, BOTHWELL ST.,
GLASGOW.
Telegraphic Address—" CARSWELL, GLASGOW

TRADE NOTES.

There is nothing startlingly fresh in the experience of the trade this week. The same steady activity prevails, prices all round remain remarkably firm, and the outward consignments show a pleasing business doing, and making ample room for the late arrivals now coming to hand.

The stocks of Baltic goods have been somewhat added to this week by a considerable number of arrivals. At Leith several cargoes have been landed, amongst them a 500 standard steamer cargo of white deals from Riga, for Garland & Roger. Messrs. John Mitchell & Co., D. W. Beattie, and Thos. M. Summers & Co. are also consignees of several Swedish and Russian cargoes.

The stock of Quebec timber at Leith has already got reduced to small proportions, and only a few cargoes are expected this fall. This, taken in conjunction with the limited Clyde stocks, will very materially affect the market during the winter and spring months.

Granton Harbour presents a quiet aspect as regards timber imports this week. We understand a cargo of Quebec timber is daily expected there, which, looking at the old stocks of this wood, is much wanted.

We direct the attention of our readers in the home-grown trade to several heavy lots announced for sale in our advertising columns. They are all extensive, and at

MR. JAMES DONALDSON (OF JAMES DONALDSON & SON, TAYPORT).

this time are worthy of the notice of large buyers.

An exceptional briskness prevails in the iron and steel manufacturing districts. In the course of visits there we find that on all hands manufacturers have orders sufficient to last well into the months of next year, and that their powers of production are put to the utmost capacity. The influence that this

Auction Sales see next page.

industry bears on the timber trade places satisfactory prospects before timber merchants.

Grangemouth Dock has resumed its activity during the last week by a considerable number of timber arrivals; we notice two steamers discharging, as well as several sailing vessels. Cronstadt, Riga, Archangel, and Swedish goods are all represented in these imports, which are having the effect of increasing the appearance of the stocks for the moment.

Quite a number of vessels have come to hand at Borrowstounness with pit props from several ports. The stocks, which were low for this season, begin to assume a more formidable appearance. The outgoing trade in these, however, keeps up well, which will prevent any undue accumulation.

We understand that the question of the non-fulfilment of contracts on the part of certain shippers has in several cases been satisfactorily arranged. It is always gratifying to learn that such disputes can be adjusted without the intervention of law.

A commencement has now been made in a few districts in the felling of home-grown timber; new wood will not, of course, be plentiful for a few weeks yet. The good existing demand, and the favourable prospects of its continuance, diminishes any chance of relaxation in the still stiffening prices of all classes of hard wood.

The Scotch Supplement of the Timber Trades Journal *in October 1888 was crowded with advertisements for Scottish timber merchants, importers and agents, including James Donaldson.*

The family tradition of naming the two elder sons James and George began with the birth of John's sons: James, born in 1791, and George, born in 1797. George became a master joiner in the village of Balbeggie, not far from Dalreitchmoor. James followed his father and spent several years working as a hand-loom weaver. But change was coming. A way of life that had remained the same for generations was being swept aside by the tide of relentless change ushering in the world's first industrialised nation. By the 1820s, when James was in his prime, the cottage industry of the hand-loom weavers was being replaced by the faster, more efficient power-looms, which were housed in the new factories that were springing up in towns and cities all over the country. This revolution brought misery and poverty to many thousands of hand-loom weavers, who suddenly found themselves destitute and unwanted. James was undeterred and more determined. He became a farmer, leasing a small farm called Whitemyre, which had a hundred acres of land.

For James Donaldson's two sons, George, born in 1818, and James, born in 1826, the consequences of Britain's Industrial Revolution would be quite different.

The two brothers recognised the potential of the timber trade almost simultaneously. After working as an engineer and millwright in Perth, George set up on his own as a wood merchant and sawmiller. For a while he formed a partnership with another sawmiller, George Leighton Robertson, trading as Robertson Donaldson & Company. Robertson appears to have occupied a sawmill and woodyards at Ferry-Port-on-Craig, as Tayport was known until the late nineteenth century, previously operated by David Spence from 1850 until 1857. On 5 May 1859, however, most of the

The Victorian Timber Industry

By the time George Donaldson was born, demand for timber was already outstripping home-grown supplies. Hardwood forests, once common in many parts of the country, had been harvested to meet the needs of Britain's navy and merchant marine. This included Scottish plantations established as part of estate 'improvements' during the eighteenth century. As a result, Britain was already a major timber importer by 1800. Imports multiplied four and a half times between 1790 and 1831 and then tripled over the ensuing fifteen years. This rapid rise from 35 million cubic feet to 100 million cubic feet occurred partly because the high duties imposed on imported Baltic timber during the Napoleonic wars were reduced in 1835 to the same level as those on imported colonial timber.

Another reason was the increasing pace of industrial change. By 1830, manufacturing already accounted for a greater share of national income than agriculture. The rate of expansion was breathtaking. In 1750, 5 million tonnes of coal were extracted from British mines. This rose to 30 million tonnes by 1830 and 117 million by 1874. The first railway was opened in 1825, and by 1850, as railway mania was just beginning to strike Scotland, Britain already boasted more than 6,000 miles of railway track. By then, iron manufacturing was just beginning to get into its stride, while steelmaking had barely started. The population was growing at an unprecedented rate, increasing from 11 million in 1800 to 37 million in 1900. Towns and cities grew rapidly to accommodate more people and expanding industries. Glasgow's population, for instance, increased in size from 77,000 people in 1800 to 400,000 in 1850. And there was more to come.

As a result of such change, Victorian Britain was profligate in its consumption of timber. Wooden sailing ships were replaced – but only slowly – by steamers made from iron and steel, while railway carriages and wagons consumed hardwood, and pine was used for countless railway sleepers. Load upon load of timber was despatched to the mines for making pit props. Timber went into every additional house built for the growing population, every shop and factory. It was in demand from glassmakers, iron-smelters and alkali-producers. To feed this consumption, greater numbers of larger ships brought back bigger volumes of better timber from all over the world. Agencies sprang up to smooth the shipment of timber from suppliers to importers and merchants. Some of the grandest agents were founded during this period, such as Churchill & Sim, Foy Morgan & Co, Price & Pierce, and William Brandt's'. On the east and west coasts of Scotland, ports imported timber from Russia and Scandinavia, the East and West Indies, Canada and the United States. Sawmills were established at many of these ports, and the railways made it possible to deliver imported timber almost anywhere.

mill machinery was sold by public auction, and the site seems to have been idle for a while until Robertson Donaldson began using the sawmill, but not the woodyards, again.

When Robertson decided to withdraw from the partnership, George invited his brother, James, to join him. For most of the 1850s, James had been running his own wood merchant's business in Corsock in Kirkcudbright. He arrived in Tayport with his wife, Catherine, and his young family, which would eventually extend to seven children. (From his second marriage, following Catherine's death, came another seven boys and girls.) The new partnership, James later recorded, began on 28 September 1860, but it was only on 23 May 1861 that the brothers placed a notice in the *Fife Herald*, announcing that 'as lessees of the concern at Tayport, we have now taken the Sawmills into our own hands, and that the business carried on there for the past twelve months by Messrs Robertson Donaldson & Co of Perth, is now taken by us, and carried on in all its departments by us, as Timber Merchants and importers for our own behoof, under the firm of G & J Donaldson'. James very quickly took the leading role in building up the Tayport business. Part of the capital he invested in the partnership came as a loan from his father, who was still owed £421 8s 2d by his son on his death in 1864.

Floating logs down river. Nineteenth century forestry work in Värmland, a historical province or landskap in the west of middle Sweden. (Alamy)

George Donaldson and His Family

George Donaldson was a businessman whose ambition outstripped his ability. In 1863 he set up his own timber firm with two of his sons, also called James and George, in South Alloa. James didn't stay with the business long, leaving in his twenties to set up his own timber business, with offices in Perth and London. Outwardly, the South Alloa business, now trading as George Donaldson & Son, seemed successful. By 1871, it was employing fifty people, with an office in Glasgow, and George was giving it his full attention, having given up his partnership in the Tayport business. But the business began to struggle, and George borrowed from his family to keep it going. When these funds ran out, a desperate George resorted to fraud, discovered after he paid one of his creditors with a worthless bill. George was bailed to appear in court in Stirling in September 1875, but his family went to great lengths to help him escape from justice. George jumped bail and took a ship for the US, heading for Canada, where the family had taken a lease on a ranch. There George spent two years before disappearing completely, never to be heard of again. Meanwhile, back in Scotland, his son George was jailed for nine months, while the younger boy, James, went bankrupt just two years after his father vanished.

> James Donaldson was a shrewd and capable businessman.

Unlike his brother, James Donaldson was a shrewd and capable businessman. The Tayport business was in safe hands. Throughout the 1860s, James built up the business by adding of bits and pieces of property. It was complex to manage because of the customs duties on imported timber, which involved a mountain of paperwork, with cash set aside to cover the duties, and a secure compound, surrounded by a 10-foot-high fence, to store the timber while it was still in bond. All this ended in 1866 when Gladstone abolished all the duties on timber, giving a huge boost to the trade in Scandinavian and Baltic timber. James certainly felt confident, buying the freehold of the sawmill and woodyards in the same year. By 1873, Sweden had taken over from Canada as the leading exporter of timber to the United Kingdom, only for Russia to assume the same position just two years later.

Timber Stock and Customers

James Donaldson imported a wide variety of timber. His stock consisted mainly of red- and white-wood deals and battens from Scandinavia, Russia and the Baltic. But Tayport also saw the arrival of timber from the west as well as the east, notably yellow pine from Quebec and pitch pine from the Gulf of Mexico. Both were much in demand, with softwoods increasingly used for housebuilding in place of heavy, scarce and expensive hardwoods. Pitch pine was popular for church and house interiors, and sawn pitch pine made good pit props. James did keep a stock of hardwoods, including Stettin oak, American oak, ash, birch and mahogany, for local customers, including builders, wheelwrights, carpenters and joiners. The firm supplied the Distillers' Company at Cameron Bridge, the Guardbridge Paper Company and a long list of colliery companies. Most customers were local, from Arbroath, Cupar, Dundee, Kirkcaldy and St Andrews, with several based in Glasgow.

Although the prospects for Scandinavian and Baltic timber attracted many new entrants to the timber trade, James Donaldson was well placed to fight the competition. Tayport's flat beach was ideal for rafting and storing logs shipped to the port. The harbour, built by the railway company, would soon be free from the ferries that carried railway passengers across the Tay, since an Act of Parliament had been passed in 1870 to build a bridge over the river, opening up Dundee for the firm. At the same time, the railway covered most of the Fife coast. The firm could import Baltic timber without hindrance and could despatch with ease orders to customers in its hinterland.

During the first half of the 1870s, the timber trade enjoyed a brief boom as the Franco-Prussian War drove up prices. After 1875, there was a prolonged depression, lasting almost until the end of the century. Business was unpredictable with profits varying wildly from one year to the next, but the firm made only one small loss, in 1879, throughout the late 1870s and early 1880s. James was able to invest steadily in new sheds and new machinery. There were saws and saw benches;

hooks, ropes, rafting chains and anchors; jankers, chains, carts, handcarts, wheelbarrows and two horses (value £140). James Donaldson had shares in three sailing vessels that brought in timber from the Baltic. In a depressed market, the value of the timber stocks held by the firm doubled over this period.

In such a volatile market, writing down the value of stocks was not unusual, as the Tayport stock books for this period illustrate. It was necessary to carry significant stocks since most timber-exporting ports could expect to be ice-bound for the first half of the year and importers had to have enough timber to see them through to the new season. By now the trade was adopting a standard measurement, the St Petersburg Standard, for the first time. Originally consisting of 120 pieces of timber measuring 12 feet by 11 inches by 1½ inches, this amounted to 165 cubic feet or 1,980 feet super. In the words of one of James Donaldson's descendants, 'a more insane unit than 165 cubic feet can hardly be imagined and it is often wondered how anything so impractical came to be adopted'.

'Some Pretty Large Transactions'

The Growth of the Partnership 1889–1917

2

The small port of Leven lay to the east of Kirkcaldy on the Firth of Forth. A small quay had replaced the natural harbour in 1821, but it was the expansion of coal mining in Fife in the last quarter of the nineteenth century that brought the port prosperity. This was largely thanks to the local landowner, R G E Wemyss, who built a new dock at Methil in 1887. He did so on the back of guarantees from his principal tenants, both involved in mining, that they would ship a certain tonnage of coal from the port every year. Britain was sending coal all over the world, and Methil became the most important coal-shipping port in Scotland. A second dock was completed in 1899 and a third in 1913, by which time the export trade in coal was in decline.

James Donaldson and his sons quickly recognised the potential for expanding sales in that part of Fife. The problem, according to his younger son, George, was that the firm 'found it a difficult matter, because of the heavy carriage, to compete with firms resident on the south side of the Forth'. It was only after they had failed to find a suitable site in Burntisland that they turned their attention to Leven and Methil. By the time the firm had been approached to buy Leven sawmills at the end of 1889, both the port and the local coal mining industry were entering their most prosperous period. The former provided Donaldson's with excellent facilities for receiving imported timber; and the latter, a ready-made and extensive market. On 19 December 1889, John Balfour & Company offered Leven sawmills to the firm for £600, an offer accepted within twenty-four hours. (More than seventy years later, the same company sold Donaldson's its second site in Leven.) At the same time,

Leven in the 1870s is depicted in the watercolour while the photograph shows the same scene after the completion of the railway siding and dock works in 1880. More importantly, the timber stacks of Donaldson's Wemyss sawmill and timber yard can be seen clearly on the left hand side in the photograph. (Painting courtesy of Colin Donaldson)

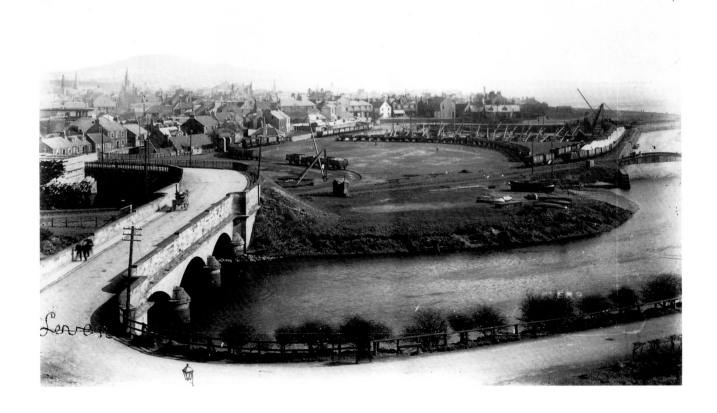

the partners negotiated acceptable rates with the North British Railway for the hauling of timber from Methil docks to the sawmills.

A month later, James Donaldson was dead. His death at the age of sixty-two was sudden and unexpected. As senior partner, his stake in the business was worth nearly £16,000, which in current values would be equivalent to nearly £2 million. His sons, James and George, became equal partners, James managing business in Tayport and George running activities in Leven. They operated almost entirely as separate businesses with their own books of account, the profits divided equally between the partners at the end of each year. The correspondence between each office was conducted on the most formal terms. In the 1890s, there was some justification for this arrangement, given the difficulties of travelling between the two yards; however, Tayport and Leven continued to be run separately, with all the duplication that was involved, until the late 1960s.

Leven, like Tayport, supplied mainly local customers, in places such as Markinch, Largo, Buckhaven, Ladybank and Dunfermline, and there was some overlap in terms of geographical coverage with Tayport. During the early 1890s, while Leven held larger stocks than Tayport, annual sales were roughly the same. In 1894, for example, sales made by the Tayport business totalled £30,784, while Leven's turnover was £32,152. In the same year, Leven made twice as much money as Tayport, achieving a net return on sales of slightly more than 8%. Tayport, on the other hand, largely funded not only the working capital that Leven needed for acceptances and cash advances on freights and cargoes but also most of its capital improvements.

The private account book kept by the partners shows how rapidly business expanded at Leven. Until the First World War, Leven tended to carry larger stocks than Tayport did. The profits, although not the sales, made by each business are recorded and, taking the figures at face value, Leven rapidly outstripped Tayport. The aggregate profits made at Leven between 1892 and 93 and between 1913 and 14 totalled £73,260 by comparison with Tayport's £11,300. Timber prices were stable for most of this period, the exception being during the time of the Boer War, when increased demand forced prices up. The firm took a cautious approach to buying. With prices beginning to rise at the end of 1899, correspondence from the Tayport office noted that 'in view of the numerous old contracts we have to implement and the excited state of the market we have been declining to enter into new arrangements'. In January 1900, writing to ship-brokers Christian Salvesen to reject offers of white wood from Norway and Latvia, Donaldson's questioned whether '… Riga shippers are doing much, if any, business at their asking prices for sawn goods'. Another offer for pine deals was turned down in June 1900 with the response that 'we have not got our customers hereabouts properly schooled yet to pay the extreme prices shippers are putting on their stocks'. Once the war ended, prices settled down again, and the price per standard of Swedish deals was the same in 1913 as it had been in 1900.

A lot of time was spent negotiating with shippers, agents and brokers, via telegram, letter and postcard. As well as Scottish agents and brokers, the firm also dealt with agents and brokers in the major English ports, including Liverpool and London. The first entry in the firm's shipping register, dated 3 November 1909, relates to 900 loads of fresh sawn timber and 45 standards of

Customer Relationships

During the early 1900s, typical customers included shipbuilders, such as the Caledon company in Dundee, boat builders, house builders, joiners, firewood merchants and sawmills. The firm received one small consignment of logs for sawing into lengths from a golf-club maker in St Andrews. (In later years, the firm supplied cut hickory to St Andrews for making reproduction putters.) The firm did a good trade with railway-wagon and carriage manufacturers and sent timber for sleepers to railway depots all over Scotland. Dundee's bobbin mills bought timber from Donaldson's. Although most customers were local, orders were occasionally despatched south of the border to places such as Sunderland.

While most customers paid their bills promptly, sometimes the accounts department had to chase up smaller customers. Judging from the frequent reminders sent out, joiners appeared to be the worst offenders. One joiner in Carnoustie deliberately stayed away when the firm's Mr Middleton called to collect his payment, resulting in an ultimatum of immediate settlement or legal action. This was an extreme example, and the firm tended to take a generous approach towards regular customers, sometimes making small loans to tide them over for a month or so before the loan and the outstanding account were expected to be repaid.

The firm responded promptly to customer complaints it considered justified, swiftly settling problems and promising better service. When a Kelty joiner had to pay extra carriage on a lot purchased at one of the firm's regular timber auctions (as important for sales at this time as individual orders) because Donaldson's had not carried out his instructions properly, the firm quickly gave him credit. The firm liked to foster long-term relationships with customers and disliked supplying timber to non-trade customers. Writing to one established customer, a Gauldry joiner called Walter Scott, in 1905, the firm noted: 'We have been asked by a Mr Johnston, Watchmaker, Dundee, to send him an estimate for some wood required in altering an old house at Gauldry. We do not encourage this sort of thing, preferring that such enquiries come through a regular customer. We have accordingly put a little on the prices, and if he sends us an order, we will credit your account with the difference. This is, of course, confidential.'

prime boards due to be delivered to Tayport from New Orleans in the spring of 1910. Since cargoes like this were shipped across the Atlantic in vessels too large for either Methil or Tayport, they were delivered directly to the firm from larger ports such as Glasgow and Dundee. Orders were divided between those marked 'Prompt' and those for shipment several months hence. Deals, battens and scantlings were principally red and white wood imported from Scandinavian, Baltic and Russian ports, such as St Petersburg, Riga, Kronstadt, Libau (now known as Liepāja in Latvia), Lillesand, Jakobstad and Archangel. The firm also imported other timber from the same ports as well as from Pensacola and New Orleans in the US and Montreal and Quebec in Canada.

Three images of timber stacked at Tayport. In the first, a horse, the main provider of motive power in the yards for many years, stands on the right. The precisely built stacks in the second show on the highest stacks to the left the projecting lengths of timber used to scale the stack when timber was brought down. The third image is a more general view of the site.

A team of Swedish lumberjacks in 1908. The logs are transported by horse and sled to the sawmill. (Alamy)

Before the First World War, sailing vessels as well as steamers continued to ship timber to Tayport and Methil. Shipping instructions drawn up by the firm were very specific. In January 1911, an order was placed through Price & Pierce in London for timber and lumber loading not later than mid-May 1911 bound from Pensacola. The first part of the discharge was intended for Methil; the second, for Tayport. The firm instructed: 'The parcel for Tayport to be loaded separately in steamer from the parcel for Methil. The whole of the lumber to be shipped under deck and to be stowed in such a manner as to avoid any damage from the Timber. Log Timber to be used for deck load.'

Once the timber arrived in port, it was discharged. This could be done only by hand, piece by piece, and not just once but four times: firstly, from the ship onto the dock side; secondly, from the dock side into the railway wagons (having sorted out all the different qualities); thirdly, from the wagons onto horse-drawn bogies; and fourthly, from the bogies into the firm's sheds. Every importer was determined that no space should be wasted on a chartered vessel, and pieces of timber occupied every nook and cranny. The first task of the stevedores was to use their boat hooks to collect the timber together in parcels, which were then swung over the side by the ship's derrick onto the quay. The movement of timber from vessel to yard did not necessarily take place at the same time;

Fifty years after the firm began trading in Tayport, James Donaldson & Sons celebrated with a jubilee auction and dinner on Wednesday, 28 September 1910. More than 200 people, including customers from all over Scotland, attended the event. The auction, which began at Tayport sawmills after the arrival of the 10.22 am train from the south, featured 'an extensive and varied assortment of timber'. After the sale finished, at around 3.30 pm, a dinner was held in Tayport's Drill Hall. Customers regarded James and George Donaldson and their firm with such respect that they had raised funds for a presentation and, on the night, the two brothers were presented with a pair of superb inscribed silver rose bowls.

The notice of the Jubilee Sale held at the Tayport mill on 28 September 1910 is accompanied by a group photograph of the customers who attended. The rose bowls they presented to the firm on the day are still displayed at every Annual General Meeting. The photograph shows (tenth and eleventh from the left in the front row) James and George Donaldson.

in particular, removing the timber from the dock side to the timber yard depended on when the importer was able to secure the wagons needed from the railway company. In 1898, the stevedoring contract at Methil was placed with Peter Stewart, who promised that he 'will always see that plenty of men are put on to receive from the various vessels in order that no detention to them during discharge is incurred by me. I also take in hand to load up the various cargoes on to wagons with the utmost despatch and will even when necessary put on men after usual working hours to do so. I will also see to the rafts of Log Timber which may be placed in Dock until such time as the Logs are lifted by me onto wagons.' As the contract makes clear,

George Donaldson and Jean Cochrane on their wedding day in 1895.

Two enchanting photographs, one of them with their mother, of the two sons of George and Jean Donaldson: the elder is Victor, born in 1898, and the younger, swathed in frills of linen and lace, is Reg, born in 1902.

making sure there was enough labour at the right rate at the right time was critical. The process was already long enough without incurring further delays, either because there were not enough men or because they were too expensive. Railway costs were a significant part of the firm's expenditure, and there were frequent arguments with the North British Railway over rates and shunting arrangements. The issue of rail freight charges was so sensitive for the industry that it had led directly to the formation of the Timber Trade Federation in 1892.

Technical breakthroughs helped to improve the productivity of the Tayport and Leven sawmills. By 1900,

the modern band-mill had been developed, enabling the wholesale production of sawn lumber. Planing machines were improved, and the introduction of cylindrical cutter-heads permitted moulding machines to operate at faster speeds. In the US and the UK, the first primitive drying kilns appeared.

James had married Mary McCulloch, but they had no children, and Mary's early death left James a widower for the last twenty years of his life. George married Jean Cochrane in 1895 and they had two sons: George Victor, born in 1897, and James Reginald, born in 1902, who were always known by their second names. Both partners lived well: in April 1913 their

Victor Donaldson at War

As a young officer, Victor inspired devotion from his soldiers. His former batman, Private Henderson, wrote to Victor's mother in June 1916: 'It was indeed a pleasure to serve such a manly young officer, none so gallant or brave as he is in this camp … please pass on my best wishes to the officer I would serve with my life, your dear son Victor, may God protect and restore him safe to his loved ones.' Victor was only eighteen years of age.

He celebrated his nineteenth birthday in billets on 22 June 1916 and later wrote home that 'I leave billets this afternoon for the trenches, I expect to be in for a spell of about twelve days. It will be a great and interesting experience for me.' In his first action he was seriously wounded. He was able to write to his mother on 3 July with a description of the incident: '…it was about 2.30 on Monday morning, the German grenade landed about a yard behind me; luckily it burst but I caught all the shrapnel below the knee. A friend who was a few yards behind me was also hit with some shrapnel

about the head and neck, but he very pluckily carried me about 100 yards through heavy fire on his back to a place of safety.' Victor's commanding officer later wrote to Mrs Donaldson: 'The man who carried him along the trench just after he was hit is being recommended for a distinction. The man himself was badly hit and has since lost his right eye. It was certainly a good deed of the man who carried Victor as it was done under very heavy shellfire, also many bombs and mortars were coming over. The man passed me with Victor on his back and they both got to a place of safety.' Victor was eventually transferred to the Yorkhill Hospital in Glasgow, where he convalesced. His serious leg injuries troubled him throughout his life but he was able to return to France where he commanded troop trains for the rest of the war.

Above: Victor Donaldson in uniform at home at the beginning of the First World War.

Left: The group photograph shows Victor Donaldson on his return to active service as a troop train commander after his convalescence. The date is 23 March 1919 and the train is the express from Boulogne to Cologne.

A cargo of unloaded timber lies next to the ship docked in Tayport harbour. The second image shows Russian timber being loaded onto the Herold tied up in the harbour at Archangel in the early 1900s. (Second image, Alamy)

Архангельскъ. — Archangel.
Лѣсная биржа Стюардъ.

capital accounts stood at nearly £50,000 each and they had each drawn the equivalent today of £115,000 each during the previous year.

The success of the business owed much to the complementary working relationship between the two brothers, who were genially competitive. This even extended to their politics. James was a staunch Liberal while George was an unswerving supporter of the Conservatives. Under the law as it then stood, they were both entitled to two votes, a residential vote and a business vote. The brothers had a mutual understanding. Each of them would vote at their respective homes in the morning. In the afternoon, after meeting for lunch at the Peat Inn, George travelled to Tayport; and James, to Leven, to cast their second votes, effectively cancelling each other out.

James died in March 1913 in his fifty-ninth year. Following the example of his father, he had taken a keen interest in local affairs. He was chairman of the parish council in Tayport, a justice of the peace for Fife and a county councillor. He was an elder, session clerk and treasurer of the Erskine United Free Church and secretary of the Tayport branch of the Scottish Bible Society. An enthusiastic sportsman, he was a member of the Scotscraig Tennis Club, of which he was president, and the Scotscraig Golf Club. He had also been president of the local Reading & Recreation Association.

James left £240 to be shared by his employees, with the rest of his estate divided between his brother and sisters. A year after his brother's death, George welcomed his elder son, Victor, into the firm. Only months later, Victor was commissioned as a lieutenant in the Black Watch, enduring a year of what he later described as 'being bullied around the yard for eight shillings a week' before marching off to war.

In the summer of 1914, a cargo of seventy standards of white wood from Finland was delivered half to Tayport and half to Methil. The order had been placed in November 1913, but against orders placed a month or more later the phrase 'Balance cancelled through the war' began to appear more frequently in the firm's shipping register. Prices were completely uncontrolled and began to rise steeply. In August 1915, the firm told the Guardbridge Paper Company that 'owing to further heavy increases in the landed value of Timber, caused by abnormally high Freights, etc., we regret it is impossible for us to continue at the rates we have been charging'. Supplies were becoming scarce. Colombian Pine was a case in point and customers switched instead to mild pitch pine or Roi Cypress.

George Donaldson did well from the war. The firm benefited, for example, from 'some pretty large transactions' with a London firm for timber for government hutting in 1914–15. Tayport and Leven

> *The success of the business owed much to the complementary working relationship between the two brothers*

> *'Balance cancelled through the war'*

made total profits of more than £87,000 between 1914 and 1919, returning almost £25,500 to the government as Excess Profits Duty. In five years, the firm made more money than in the previous twenty, and even taking taxation into account the return was handsome.

Throughout 1915 the firm continued to receive timber from Russia, principally from Archangel, as well as from North America. But conditions were becoming more severe. The Germans were blockading the Baltic. In September that year a vessel chartered by the firm was sunk en route to collect cargo, and a replacement had to be sought. There was a shortage of labour. In October 1915, a letter from the firm noted that 'within the last week we have had three steamer cargoes discharging at Tayport and owing to the great dearth of labour we had to close down the mill for a few days, employing every one of our hands at the Harbour'. Then came the unstable political situation in Russia, culminating in the Revolution, which brought a halt for some time to supplies of timber from either Russia or Finland.

Events forced the government's hand. A leading member of the industry, Montague Meyer, was appointed Timber Buyer with responsibility for all national requirements. In 1917, James Ball became Timber Controller, fixing maximum selling prices. At the end of May 1917, James Donaldson & Sons wrote to one customer that 'quantities under a standard, up to 1% of our stock, is all we are allowed to dispose of without a Permit and as a large proportion of our stock has been requisitioned by the government we regret we cannot make you a definite offer as to when we can execute and deliver any order'. The firm bought home-grown timber, as foreign timber was rationed, but much of it was suitable only for pit-wood, although the firm could say in December 1917 that it was 'very busy among Homewood boarding and Scantlings'.

'Uncertain Conditions'

Inter-war Difficulties 1917–39

3

With one son on active service and the other too young, George Donaldson remained in sole charge during the war. Always immaculately dressed, he was driven around by his chauffeur, William Thompson, in a Daimler car, which bore his monogram. Its number, SP3, indicated that an earlier Donaldson vehicle was one of the first to be registered in Fife. One of George's grandchildren remembered journeying in the car with his grandmother. There was a glass partition between the driver and the rear passengers, with communication through an inter-connecting phone. As soon as Mrs Donaldson felt Thompson was exceeding thirty miles an hour, she would pick up the phone and say, 'Thompson, not so fast, please!'

Although George Donaldson was respected by his workforce, for many of them he was an austere, distant and forbidding figure. He insisted on checking all newly stacked timber, and if trade markings were not the right way up, he had the stack re-built.

When the war finally ended, there was a huge pent-up demand for timber. Large stocks were sold between 1919 and 1921 through a government firm, Associated Importers Ltd, made up of most of the major importers. But with normal sources of supply, notably Russia, still disrupted, government stocks were in such demand that prices, which were no longer controlled, shot up. During the war, prices paid by Donaldson's for a standard of red wood or white wood had ranged between £9 10s and £23 15s; in 1919 prices varied from £27 to £43 10s and in 1920 reached £55 per standard for some qualities and sizes.

The boom did not last. Between 1919 and 1921, Donaldson's sales averaged £209,000, but in 1922 they dropped to £139,000. Profits varied even more, collapsing from £9,000 in 1920 to a loss of more than £21,000 in 1921 as the average price per standard of timber halved from £40 to £20, ruining many merchants. As a result of the slump, the government granted large rebates on agreed prices for government stocks, helping to foster a steady recovery, and price settled around wartime levels for the rest of the 1920s.

Perhaps it was the prospect of a slump that convinced George Donaldson in 1919, when the firm was making record sales and profits, that the time had come to convert the partnership into a limited liability company as James Donaldson & Sons Ltd. George Donaldson received £3,628 0s 6½d in cash and seven thousand £10 shares. William Reid, the commercial manager at Leven, was appointed to the board, the first non-family member to become a director. It seems unlikely that he exercised much real influence; his appointment was mainly to provide a necessary second director, given Victor's absence and Reginald's youth. Alexander Watt took the post of secretary. David Donaldson, a son of the founder from his second marriage, was works manager at Tayport; and James McPherson, works manager at Leven.

It was George Donaldson who first gave employees the chance to own shares in the business, an initiative the company has continued ever since. Reid, Watt, David Donaldson, McPherson and another employee, David Smith, one of the firm's commercial travellers, all accepted the invitation to take up shares. Reid invested more than £2,000; and McPherson, £1,000. These were considerable sums and George Donaldson may have given them financial help.

William Reid became the company's first non-family director in 1919.

It was George Donaldson who first gave employees the chance to own shares in the business

In 1923, Victor Donaldson, who was running Leven, joined the board. Shrewd and level-headed, he gradually began to take over a greater share of the buying duties from his father, who still had the final say. Victor married Jean Robertson, granddaughter of the founder of the Robertson 'Golden Shred' marmalade empire in Paisley. They had met at Yorkhill, where Jean's brother had been the patient in the bed next to Victor. After a long engagement, the couple married in 1925 and had three children, George, Jean and Valerie. A great family man,

Victor (1) and Reg (2) Donaldson as young men. While Victor was responsible for the business as a whole, each of the brothers ran their own branches as individual businesses, Victor at Leven and Reg at Tayport. Very different personalities, they complemented each other and worked well together in business.

The next generation, a photograph taken at Stanely, Lundin Links, in 1937: (left to right) (back row) Mrs Webster (who looked after Victor's children following the death of their mother in 1935); George R Donaldson, Reg's eldest son and later one of Donaldson's first non-executive directors; the local minister, Mr Dempster; Bill Donaldson, Reg's second son, later headmaster of Newcastle-under-Lyme Grammar School; Mrs George Donaldson; (front row) Colin Donaldson, Reg's youngest son, later Donaldson's sales director; Jean Donaldson, Victor's elder daughter and a talented artist; George N Donaldson, Victor's son, later the company's chairman; and Valerie Donaldson, Victor's younger daughter.

Victor was very approachable outside work. Brought up to be correct, proper and well-dressed, he was quite shy, which could make him seem distant to his employees, who nevertheless respected his honesty and integrity.

Victor's brother, Reginald, known as Reg, joined the firm in 1921 and became a director in 1927. He took charge of Tayport and looked after the company's larger customers. Fun-loving and gregarious, warm and personable, he was a born salesman, disliking routine and loving contact with people. A kind and helpful man, with a great sense of humour, he could be impetuous and occasionally explosive. He knew when to be firm. A customer noted for his rough language once rang him at Tayport from Broughty Ferry across the river. His language was so crude and his voice so loud that Reg told him the telephone was quite unnecessary, he could be heard quite clearly without it, and put the phone down. Reg married Winnie Logan in 1927 and they had three sons, George, Bill and Colin.

Brothers Bill and George Donaldson, sons of Reg Donaldson, on packs of timber at Tayport.

Victor and Reg worked well together. They were great friends, and occasional differences never eroded their mutual admiration. They complemented each other in business, with Victor and his father taking care of the buying and Reg looking after sales. As their fathers had been, so each of the brothers was totally responsible for the affairs of the respective branches they managed. Victor may have been in overall charge of buying, but certain purchases at Tayport were made only by Reg. Similarly, Reg would never have dreamt of interfering with the sales office at Leven.

The brothers followed the examples of their father, uncle and grandfather in taking an active part in the lives of their local communities. Victor was an elder of St John's Church, Leven, for more than thirty years and he was a long-serving trustee of the Kirkcaldy & District Trustee Savings Bank. He was a founder member of the Leven Rotary Club and, because of the illness of one of his daughters, became deeply involved in the Fife Polio Fellowship, serving as its honorary president. He was twice president of the Leven Curling Club and a member of several local golf clubs. He was an accomplished golfer, playing for the County of Fife and competing in the British and Scottish amateur championships. Reg was an elder of his local church in Tayport, where he served as a member of the town council and as a justice of the peace. He became a director of the Guardbridge Paper Company and the Crieff Hydro. He was chairman of the Hydro's board for many years and chairman of the governors of Merchiston Castle School. A keen cricketer and rugby player, he too was a talented golfer.

During the 1920s, most timber still came from Scandinavia and the Baltic, with small amounts from North America and the new republic of Czechoslovakia.

The Great Depression left so many local men out of work that the unemployed queued up every morning outside the company's gates

In June 1923, Donaldson's completed its first post-war order from Russia for a quantity of red and white wood from Petrograd via the Russian Wood Agency Ltd. By the late 1920s, Tayport and Methil were receiving about seven or eight cargoes each season, varying in size from 120 standards upwards. The firm also bought small quantities of hardwoods, including Rangoon teak and Austrian oak.

Discharge at the ports remained labour intensive. The stevedores made up into sets the loose cargoes on board the ships. These were slung onto the shore by the ship's gear and loaded by hand onto railway wagons for discharge and stacking in the yard. They used 'donkeys' with a point on one end, which were used to 'pinch' pieces of timber up onto the stacks. It was hard physical work and the men wore leather shoulder pads to relieve the pressure of the timber they carried.

Sales and profits remained steady until 1930–31, when the company made a loss as turnover fell. Although there was plenty of timber available, there was little demand. The Great Depression left so many local men out of work that the unemployed queued up

Sawyers, Salesmen and Office Staff

When Jim Henderson joined the firm in Tayport at the age of fourteen in November 1924, he was among a dozen boys working at the moulding machines for eleven shillings a week. The sawmill started up at 7.30 am six mornings a week, stopping at 5 pm during the week and at noon on Saturdays. Christmas Day was a working day (Victor Donaldson had a habit of telephoning English customers to conclude contracts), and time off at New Year was regarded as a temporary lay-off without pay. At Leven, John Smith was paid 10s 6d a week when he took up his job, working below the saw floor, collecting chips for barrowing to the fire-hole to fuel the steam engine that drove the mill. Sawdust was bagged up and taken to Kirkcaldy once a month, where it was used to make linoleum. The firm's saw doctor, Thomas Hood, sharpened every saw by hand. Like many saw doctors, he took a pride in the secrets of his craft and refused to sharpen a saw when he was being watched.

The office in Leven was run by five staff, all of them men, with the first woman joining the staff during the Second World War. There was an unofficial uniform – the men wore plus-fours; and the office boy, short trousers. Robert Walker, the fifteen-year-old office boy in 1927, later recalled how the office staff always felt 'rather superior to the men outside'. Everything was recorded in ink. Robert was proud of his handwriting and was promoted to look after the sales book – 'It would take me all day to write up the previous day's deliveries, most of which were made by horse and cart.' A few years later, in 1934, Bob Cumming started work as the office boy

at Leven on eight shillings a week. He had left his previous employer when he was refused leave to play in the British Boys' Golf Tournament in Leeds that year. As a keen golfer, Victor Donaldson was much more sympathetic, granting him leave on this occasion and several future occasions. Bob was encouraged to learn short-hand, book-keeping and typing at night school.

Salesmen left the office early each morning, catching a train to the station nearest their customers, whom they visited on foot. There were usually two or three salesmen, including David Donaldson, who had changed his role, David Smith and John Urquhart. Covering Fife, Edinburgh, Glasgow and Stirling, they were joined in 1931 by John McGough, previously employed as a commission salesman.

every morning outside the company's gates at Tayport and Leven in the hope of being taken on to stack newly arrived timber. The company secretary wrote to one unemployed man in May 1930 to say that it was unlikely that any vacancies would arise soon. He added: 'In any case I am afraid you are a little too far advanced, as, should the occasion arise, we would look out for a youth just from school who would commence his duties as office boy. This has always been our method.'

Poor trading conditions continued until the mid-1930s. Tayport lost money from 1930 to 1932, while Leven only made one loss, in 1930–31. When the company recorded a further loss in 1935, it was attributed entirely to Tayport's poor performance, Leven having broken even. The directors noted that 'the results were a disappointment to all'; 'the volume of business has been good, but a fall in prices has caused a writing down of stocks, which has affected results at both works'.

Although plant and machinery at Leven required updating, Tayport was badly in need of modernisation. While many businesses cut back on investment during the depression, Victor and Reg did the opposite. To make sure the business benefited from the eventual

The Tayport office in March 1923 with its tall stools, high sloping desks, pens, ink-wells and hand-written ledgers. Behind the counter on the left stands John Barron, the cashier, appointed a director in 1938, and later company secretary. Third from the left in front of the typewriter is the young Reg Donaldson. In the safe on the right he locked John Barron after being refused permission to leave work early one Saturday to place cricket in Edinburgh.

upturn in the economy, they invested in both sites. New saws and high-speed planing machines were installed at Leven, while the mill at Tayport was reconstructed and re-equipped. During the work at Tayport in 1932–33, the company took advantage of slack trade to use the workforce as labourers for the contractors. Many men might otherwise have been laid off.

In 1936, Victor and Reg became joint managing directors, taking over from their father. For many years Victor was active on the executive committee of the Scottish Timber Merchants' & Sawmillers' Association, being president between 1936 and 1938. His wife, Jean, had died in 1935, and Victor would marry Mary Hendry in 1940, having two children, Mindy and Donald.

George Donaldson died in 1937 at the age of seventy-seven. His widow, Jean, a gracious and regal woman, outlived him by another twenty-four years. Victor succeeded his father as company chairman. In 1938, the brothers decided the positions of joint managing directors were unnecessary and gave up the roles. In the same year, J D Barron, formerly the cashier and now the company secretary, joined the board.

During the 1930s the long-serving works managers at Leven, James McPherson, and at Tayport, Robert Williamson, both retired. Before the war, pension schemes were rare in smaller businesses, and any pensions were paid at the discretion of the directors. Robert Williamson, for example, received monthly payments of £1 10s for the first five years of his retirement. In 1939 the directors reviewed the arrangement and, on the basis that Williamson was now receiving a state pension, agreed instead to make two payments of £5 each year.

One advance in 1939 came about when the salesman at Leven, David Smith, fell ill. The directors took the advice of Smith's doctor and 'it was agreed we should get a motor car (second-hand if possible) for his journeys and employ a man to drive'. A chauffeur was engaged for £3 a week and a 14 horse-power Vauxhall bought for £100. Soon afterwards, a car was provided for the Tayport salesman.

Although trading conditions steadily improved after 1935, partly because of a boom in housebuilding, the atmosphere was febrile and insecure. In 1937, the board noted the 'abnormal rise' in the timber market: 'The demand was strong, but Scandinavian shippers imposed quotas limiting output and production, which caused dearer timber but had the effect of regulating and stabilising the market.' With a total turnover of nearly £204,000, profits of more than £25,000 were the highest recorded since 1921–22. In real terms, given deflation since the early 1930s, this was a better result. Modernisation appeared to have had a limited impact on performance at Tayport, which made another loss in 1938 as overall profits fell by half. The minutes noted: 'With uncertain conditions prevailing, the buying policy of the board had been a conservative one. The Market was in a highly nervous condition with competition exceedingly keen.'

When stock often represented half annual sales, buying the right timber at the right price at the right time was crucial to making a profit. It was incredibly difficult, given the vagaries of the market, with often huge and rapid swings in prices, and the need to consider trade rumours and advice from agents. Buyers placed orders at intervals in autumn and winter for delivery the following summer and autumn. Importers had to make sure they had sufficient stocks to see them through the winter and spring. With few drying kilns, almost all timber on order was over-wintered and 'seasoned'. As nearly every port was ice-bound until the spring or early summer, orders were placed in the previous autumn for 'FOW' or 'First Open Water'. Since this date was unpredictable, there was frenetic activity when waters were open for the first time as suppliers desperately tried to ship their timber.

Importers usually chartered their ships through shipping agents. At the main ports regular liner services were operated by large ships supplying several different customers. At smaller ports, such as Tayport and Methil, the importer developed his own chartering expertise. This too was risky. While charters specified the date for timber shipments, they allowed the ship owner to vary this if the ship was hindered by storms or sundry other obstacles. As a result, it could be weeks or months beyond the due delivery date before the timber arrived.

The nervous state of the market continued during 1939 as prices fell and then rose sharply in response to the accelerating pace of the rearmament programme. Consequently, Baltic timber was in short supply and, noted the board at the end of August, this 'caused us to turn our attention to wood from the Pacific Coast and we had actually contracted for a direct shipment to Methil Dock'. Within days the declaration of war against Germany would transform the whole situation once again.

SAVE TIMBER!

EVERY STANDARD OF TIMBER SAVED FROM CONSUMPTION OR SALVAGED FOR RE-USE FREES SHIPPING SPACE FOR MUNITIONS OF WAR FOR THE SECOND FRONT

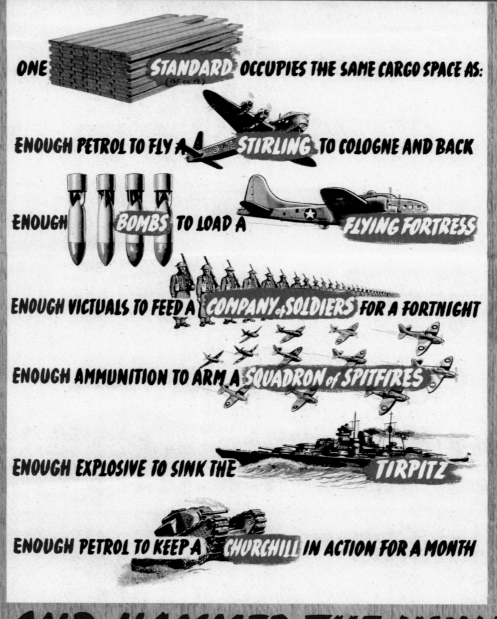

ONE **STANDARD** OCCUPIES THE SAME CARGO SPACE AS:
(165 cu. ft.)

ENOUGH PETROL TO FLY A **STIRLING** TO COLOGNE AND BACK

ENOUGH **BOMBS** TO LOAD A **FLYING FORTRESS**

ENOUGH VICTUALS TO FEED A **COMPANY of SOLDIERS** FOR A FORTNIGHT

ENOUGH AMMUNITION TO ARM A **SQUADRON of SPITFIRES**

ENOUGH EXPLOSIVE TO SINK THE **TIRPITZ**

ENOUGH PETROL TO KEEP A **CHURCHILL** IN ACTION FOR A MONTH

AND HAMMER THE HUN!

ISSUED BY TIMBER CONTROL DEPARTMENT, MINISTRY OF SUPPLY. NO. 51

'Limitations'

4

The war rapidly made an impact on James Donaldson & Sons Ltd. At Leven, John Smith recalled cutting an order soon after war broke out for two wagon-loads of battens for army billets in Shetland. The ship carrying the timber was sunk by a U-boat not far out from Methil, and the order had to be repeated.

The Timber Control was established immediately. The Ministry of Supply became the sole supplier of timber; stocks were sold at fixed maximum prices, and consumer sales were made by permit only. The country was divided into areas under area officers. Among them was Victor Donaldson, who became area officer for Area 13 covering Dundee. This experience enabled him to say later in the war that 'having seen Control from both sides, while it had limitations, on the whole we could pay an honest tribute to it having done a good job indeed for the Trade'. Initially there had been less warmth towards the Timber Control. In 1940, the directors complained that 'this all meant extra book-keeping and extra work accentuated by losing members of the staff on Service, this was being overcome ...'.

Both the Donaldson brothers served in the Home Guard. The Tayport area became a base for many Free Norwegians and Poles, fighting in exile for the freedom of their homelands; and Reg's wife, Winnie, helped to set up and run a canteen for them in the former Tayport Scout Hut.

The occupation of Norway in 1940 effectively ended supplies of Baltic timber. Canadian timber, increasingly popular before the war thanks to imperial preference, made up part of the difference, 718,000 standards being

Members of the Women's Timber Corps taking a break. (Alamy)

imported during the year. But imports were kept to a minimum as Methil and Tayport concentrated on wartime activities. Methil docks became a marshalling point for the Arctic convoys sailing to Russia, while RAF marine craft were stationed at Tayport, as Douglas Campsie, who joined the firm in October 1940 aged fifteen, remembered. Instead of imports, priority was given to harvesting home-grown timber. Ancient oaks and elms, with thousands of firs and pines, were felled by lumberjacks from around the Commonwealth and from the Women's Timber Corps. Eventually home-grown wood supplied half the country's wartime raw timber requirements.

The company applied for and received a quota for an allocation of national stock in 1940. By the beginning of the year, the company was already buying home-grown timber, including 45,000 cubic feet of spruce and fir from Messrs Jones at Larbert. Under the Timber Control, the company became wharfingers for imported timber controlled by the government. By the summer of 1941, the company's own stocks were minimal, valued at slightly more than £4,000, 'our main purpose', noted the directors, 'being the wharfinging and distribution of National Stocks'. With less invested in timber, the company's cash and financial investments stood at record levels. Profits were consistently higher than they had been in the years immediately before the war, making it possible to invest in a new electric gantry crane at Leven in late 1941. In the summer of 1942, the board stated that 'only very small quantities of imported timber remained, and we could not look for any great increase. As Sawmillers we had been fairly busy, mostly in the cutting out of Homewoods. A part of our profit was from handling and rentals for storing National Stocks.' The new crane proved inadequate for

'Alterations in ideas and in Plant may be necessary if we are to march with the times and keep up to date'

the greater volume of home-grown timber and it had been extended by mid-1943. More plant was installed at both Tayport and Leven to process more timber. Having been set up to deal with square-cut imported timber, the mills had to be altered to handle timber in the round. Throughput was important since profit margins were not as large on home-grown timber as they were on imports. To increase output, a temporary sawmill was established at Leven on 1 September 1943.

The company was determined to be ready for the return of peace, whenever that came. In December 1943, the board discussed 'the post-war position and requirements and resolved that this should have every consideration and that plans be formulated'. In the middle of June 1944, with the D-Day campaign well underway, Victor Donaldson looked ahead. He felt that greater standardisation might come from prefabrication and that timber merchants might have 'to prepare components to the stage of erection'. He concluded: 'Alterations in ideas and in Plant may be necessary if we are to march with the times and keep up to date.' Competition would mean 'a need for modern methods'. The Leven mill in particular needed modernising.

New Arrivals

As men returned from the war, the company was able to send out salesmen once more. Since David Thomson and Bob Cumming had only one car between them, their areas were modified to enable them to go out on alternate days. Robert Walker also returned to his post as cashier. One of the firm's new arrivals was Ian Johnston, who considered himself lucky to be offered a job since so many were held open for demobbed servicemen. For one pound a week, Ian followed the pattern of his predecessors as office boy. Every morning his first task was sweeping the floor; every evening his last was to bring in coal and kindling ready to prepare coal fires for the next day. He kept the time book – those more than three minutes late were 'quartered', that is, docked a quarter of an hour's pay. At night school he bettered himself by taking short-hand, book-keeping and typing. Within a year his pay had increased and he was promoted upstairs in the office to help with the day-book and pricing. Using pen, ink and blotting paper (changed every Monday), seated on a high stool at a high desk, he calculated prices to one-sixteenth of a penny.

Another new arrival was Victor Donaldson's son, George. Like his father and uncle, he was a keen sportsman, enjoying cricket, rugby and golf. He was adept at other pastimes too. A convoy sailing up the Forth was once alarmed to see what appeared to be frantic signalling coming from the shore; the policeman sent to investigate discovered young George Donaldson flying his kite. He was with the Black Watch, his father's regiment, from 1944, serving in Egypt and Palestine at the height of the post-war troubles. Joining the company in 1948, he travelled to Sweden and Finland for six months' training in 1951. In 1953 he became a director and in the same year married Fiona Todd, the daughter of the highly respected Leven doctor, Dr R W Todd. They had two children, Neil and Graham. George discovered that his father and uncle held the reins of the business very tightly in their hands. Following a pattern set by their own father, they delegated very little and kept total control over buying. They sent George to reopen the Glasgow and West of Scotland sales territory.

Peace did not bring a return to normal. The economic cost of the war resulted in a decade of retrenchment and austerity. The government created National Softwood Brokers Ltd in 1945, which distributed softwood bought by the Timber Control to importers based on individual quotas. Donaldson's was allocated its first quota, worth £52,000, at the beginning of 1946. By now, suitable home-wood trees were almost unobtainable, and the company felt that this side of the business 'must be almost written off'. Baltic supplies remained disrupted and the company was reliant upon timber from the Pacific Coast, which was not always suitable for housing. Deals, battens and logs were coming from Germany, although it was not always very good quality. John Smith remembered several saw blades were ruined because this timber was riddled with bullets and shrapnel. A mine detector was even used, without success, to identify all the metal in the wood. (Metal detectors were

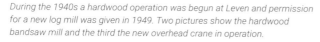

During the 1940s a hardwood operation was begun at Leven and permission for a new log mill was given in 1949. Two pictures show the hardwood bandsaw mill and the third the new overhead crane in operation.

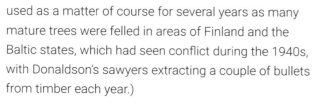

used as a matter of course for several years as many mature trees were felled in areas of Finland and the Baltic states, which had seen conflict during the 1940s, with Donaldson's sawyers extracting a couple of bullets from timber each year.)

Victor and Reg began modernising the business after the war. Their plans were hindered by the long delays in obtaining new plant and machinery commonplace at the time, but a new lighting system and new crane were installed at Tayport in 1945. More extensive plans were prepared for Leven. Difficulties in acquiring plant meant that the Leven mill still used steam power to operate its heavier plant, the steam engine fed by sawdust and wood chips shovelled in a

constant stream into the fire holes. But a new crane was ordered in 1948, and in 1949 building licences were obtained for a new log mill and saw shop, where saws were sharpened automatically. At Methil docks, timber was not only loaded directly from the ship to the railway wagons for the first time but was also discharged by mobile crane from the wagons when they reached the yard at Leven. Since mechanical stacking required more space, another yard at Burnmill in Leven was acquired and a new railway siding constructed. An agreement was signed with a local haulier for the exclusive use of one of his lorries for deliveries; otherwise, customers often sent their own transport to collect orders. At Tayport, new plant, including a planer and an automatic saw sharpener, arrived in 1951, and the yard's last horse-drawn bogie disappeared in 1952. A note in the minute book reads, 'Reported horse at Tayport was getting restless. Agreed the matter of replacing with another Tractor be gone into.' This was done although not until all the feeding stuffs had been used up.

Reducing costs was behind the streamlining of timber handling at Methil in the face of disadvantageous new terms offered by the newly nationalised British Railways. At Tayport the problem was different. With the nationalisation of the railways in 1947, responsibility for the harbour passed to the Docks & Inland Waterways Board. The harbour had been closed to commercial traffic during the war and needed dredging to remove the accumulated silt. The Board had little interest in the harbour, which was hardly used by anyone else apart from James Donaldson & Sons Ltd and occasionally the Guardbridge Paper Company, and was reluctant to spend any money on maintenance. Donaldson's constantly pressed the Board to take some responsibility for dredging the harbour. Eventually, in January 1954, the Board agreed to carry out partial dredging, but the company would bear all the costs. Even so, it was nearly another three years before dredging was completed, the company having resorted to writing to its MP.

By the late 1940s, imported softwood was still in short supply and the specification and qualities available were generally unsuitable for normal demand. With hardwoods almost free from control, the firm was developing an experimental hardwood side at Leven,

'Reported horse at Tayport was getting restless. Agreed the matter of replacing with another Tractor be gone into'

stocking, for example, largely unknown West African species. Wallboards were also freed from control, and in 1949 the company became a wallboard importer as agent for Kramfors wallboards.

From 1950, controls were gradually relaxed. Softwood importers were able to import freely on their own account from the Baltic and certain other countries, although the government continued to handle the valuable dollar timbers from the Pacific Coast. James Donaldson & Sons at once began to place forward orders for softwoods. By mid-February 1951, these totalled 1,568 standards valued at £98,000. Softwoods were released from price control although consumer licensing was maintained. In financing rising demand, Victor Donaldson was concerned about higher prices and higher freight costs. Like many other experienced timber buyers, he remembered too well the boom and bust following the removal of controls at the end of the First World War. He told his fellow directors in the summer of 1951 that 'one could not overlook a sudden fall in value, remembering what took place in 1921'. He need not have worried. Buying confidence was dampened when the government reimposed a global quota system in 1952. It would be nearly two years before the government finally relinquished control of the timber trade.

'Nervous Reactions'

A Return to the Market Place 1953–69

5

After fourteen years, state control of the timber trade was at last relinquished with the abolition of consumer licensing in November 1953. In February 1954, the directors cautiously noted that 'buying policy for early summer was under consideration and agreed we might book up to 500 standards and thereafter see how the market went'. By the following year, softwood stocks in the UK matched pre-war levels for the first time since 1945. In both 1938 and 1955, timber was the UK's most important imported raw material in terms of value.

The ending of controls stimulated a burst of intense competition. Merchants from northern England began creeping across the border to trade in Scotland. The post-war free market was just as unpredictable in the 1950s as it had been before 1939. While the British population enjoyed a sustained rise in living standards during the 1950s, accompanied by relatively low inflation and minimal unemployment, the timber trade faced uncertain prices, falling margins and keen competition. By 1960, the value of the firm's sales had fallen in real terms compared with 1951 when the first benefits of an easing of controls had been experienced. More importantly, after achieving record profits of more than £66,000 on sales of £641,000 in 1952–53, the company's profitability, excepting 1959, fell steadily. This time, compared with the inter-war years, it was Tayport rather than Leven that was more profitable.

Victor Donaldson found circumstances throughout the 1950s very trying. When prices were rising, the firm was paying higher freight rates and faced the disruption caused by striking dockers at the main English ports. This led to a scarcity of shipping, forcing Donaldson's to over-winter part of its timber purchases overseas. When prices were stable, keen competition meant 'the prices that we were able to obtain were insufficient to cover increasing on-costs plus a reasonable margin of profit'. When prices were falling, cargoes were often uneconomic to ship, the value of stocks was written down, competition intensified, and margins diminished once more. Caution was the chairman's watchword, reflected in his comments to the board in September 1958: 'I feel that an all-round reduction in stock holdings might tend to calm present nervous reactions and it is our intention to minimise purchases to a reasonable extent till this phase passes'. The firm also had to contend with the consequences of a decade of 'stop-go' national economic management. To control inflation or to support the pound, the government regularly raised the bank rate and tightened hire-purchase controls. In 1957–58, what Victor Donaldson described as 'the fantastically high rate of borrowing' cost the firm £13,500 in interest charges.

The chairman's frustration was exemplified in his report to the board in the summer of 1957: 'too many traders, some small and not too responsible, the necessity to carry heavy stocks, heavy cost of borrowing and the "credit squeeze", extended credit to customers, the temptation to absorb increasing costs such as wages, power, light and heat, postal and telephone services, transport, etc., strikes and threats of strikes – all these inflationary factors are realities which seem to receive far too little consideration'. All this, he pointed out, also applied to the timber exporting countries. Costs were rising more than prices customers were prepared to pay, leading to the devaluation of currencies, the collapse of several suppliers and the switch by several shippers from

timber to more profitable cargoes such as pulp. The situation was compounded, said the chairman, by 'Russian sales methods which had a lot to answer for'. The monolithic Russian state timber organisation forced selling prices down by flooding the market with timber. The competition was so fierce in 1958–59 that the industry suffered its worst year since the early 1930s. Swedish and Finnish shippers reported that the season had been catastrophic for sawn timber and only the profits from timber by-products saved larger firms from significant losses. In the UK, Reg Donaldson reported to his brother that consumers and contractors were taking advantage of the situation. Victor told the board that 'the Importer was carrying heavy commitments which all the time tended to depreciate in value, and eventually the Merchant who attempted to maintain selling prices, bearing some relation to cost, came off worst at the end of the day'. In that year, the firm's profits on a turnover of £575,000, depressed by falling prices, slumped to just over £8,000. Leven was barely profitable. The firm was nevertheless able to issue a reasonable dividend each year, through the existence of the dividend equalisation reserve, a fund built up during good years to enable dividends to be paid in poor years when profits were insufficient.

As well as buying cautiously, the firm was also trying to become more efficient to counter adverse conditions. In 1957, the company became the first Scottish timber company to buy a forklift truck, used to handle timber at the newly acquired 11-acre Elm Park site in Leven. Adapted to carry loads end-on, it helped to bring about an immediate improvement in productivity. It was pointed out that it would have taken eighty men before the war to handle the same amount of timber. By 1960, a second forklift truck was in use at Elm Park and there was a mobile crane for the more rapid discharge of railway wagons.

The Elm Park site had belonged to a local bonemeal mill operated by John Balfour & Sons. Purchased in 1955, it provided valuable extra space for stacking timber. To provide more under-cover storage suitable for forklift use, a former aircraft hangar from Errol aerodrome was acquired and re-erected in 1962. The yard also came with historically advantageous demurrage rates. Demurrage was in effect a fine levied on importers by the railway if they could not empty the wagons they had hired within a certain time. The bonemeal mill had originally negotiated

Above: Elm Park timber yard under snow with a Coles crane in operation, possibly the winter of 1963.

Below: Jim Cuthbert can be seen on the left showing the first Tanalith plant at Wemyss.

a low demurrage rate, and rates remained low since increases were always made in percentage terms. Each day there were two 30-wagon shunts from the docks, loaded with loose timber, dumped in lanes by the forklift trucks, sorted to size and stacked.

Very soon, however, Donaldson's abandoned rail in favour of road haulage for moving timber from the docks. The lines at Tayport and at the Wemyss mill in Leven had disappeared by the summer of 1959. When Harry Robb joined the company at Tayport in 1960, cargoes from the half a dozen or so boats unloaded in the harbour every year were taken to the yard by tractors and bogies. Two years later, faced with a demand from British Rail for an increase of 450% in railway rates, the board agreed to use road haulage for shifting timber from Methil docks to the Leven yards. On 12 April 1961, the board noted that 'a South Swedish cargo had been landed to our lorries at Methil Dock very satisfactorily and the cost shows a

considerable saving over rail transport'. Three years later, British Rail gave notice to terminate the agreement for the use of the sidings at all the Leven yards since they had not been used for some time.

In 1956, another member of the fourth generation of the family joined the firm. Colin Donaldson was Reg's youngest son. He was based at Tayport with his

Two images of the discharge of loose timber cargoes in the early 1960s – the Schleswig-Holstein at Tayport and the Anne Ohl at Methil.

> *'The one company had two identical sawmills, ran two separate sales forces, kept two sets of books – and competed fiercely to produce the best result'*

Working at Tayport

At Tayport, Colin Donaldson found a loyal and long-serving workforce, whose lives were bound up with each other in good times and bad. Many men arrived in the bothy to clock in an hour before the hooter went for the start of work at eight so they had time to exchange news with friends, read the newspapers and perhaps place a bet with one of the men who supplemented his wage through commission as a betting agent. Among the many skilled men, the most important were the saw doctor, sawyers and machine men, who had all served at least four years as apprentices. Many were great characters, like Peter Williamson and Hugh Ross, Chic and Ernie Hill, 'Big' Dave McBay and Jim Lindsay. Andrew Samuel, a labourer who worked forty-five years with the firm, had served in the same platoon as Victor Donaldson during the First World War and was close by him when he was wounded.

father and after spending several months in Sweden in 1957 moved onto sales. In that year, John Barron retired through ill-health after nearly twenty years on the board, the chairman emphasising 'his sterling qualities of industry and integrity'. Robert Walker took over as company secretary. Colin Donaldson joined the board in 1964.

Of the firm in the late 1950s, George Donaldson later wrote that 'the one company had two identical sawmills, ran two separate sales forces, kept two sets of books – and competed fiercely to produce the best result'. There was a gentleman's understanding that North Fife, Dundee, Perth and Angus were Tayport territory (but not north of Montrose, which was ceded to Fleming's), whereas Leven, which had built up a good business supplying the mining townships in the Fife coalfield, began to spread further south and west, into the Lothians and through to Glasgow.

One of the Tayport salesmen was Douglas Campsie. Most of his customers, whom he visited every fortnight, were small joiners, but they also included boat builders, coach builders, ladder manufacturers and industrial firms. He posted his day's orders at 8.15 pm in the evening and they arrived at Tayport by first post the next morning. Andy Waddell, who joined as an office boy at Leven in

1960, remembered that every price (still calculated in sixteenths of a penny) quoted to a customer over the telephone had to be confirmed in writing. Because most customers were small, the lorries from Leven made up to twenty deliveries between Leven and Glasgow, some no larger than twenty pieces of timber. No order was too small. Local joiners often brought their wheelbarrows to fill up at the mill. They settled their account perhaps twice a year, regarding it as a social occasion over which to have a cup of tea and twenty minutes' chat.

Changes were badly needed in the way the business was managed. The first came in 1957 when the accounts and book-keeping for both Tayport

The Donaldson board and senior staff during the centenary year in 1960: (left to right) (back row) Ian Johnston, Alec Herd, Bill Cunningham, Jim Cuthbert, Ron Dickson, Jock Hastie, Bob Curry, Bob Cumming; (front row) John McRae, Colin Donaldson, Reg Donaldson, Victor Donaldson, George Donaldson, Robert Walker and Dave Main.

and Leven were centralised at Leven. Pressure from George Donaldson led the board to appoint consultants in 1959 to investigate management control and yard administration at Leven, which resulted in the introduction of an incentive scheme. (The fact that Tayport was managed independently of Leven meant that a similar scheme was not introduced there until 1968.) Working conditions were improved. Machinists and labourers had been granted paid holidays for the first time in 1952. In 1959 a sick-pay scheme for employees and staff was introduced. A five-day working week became effective from April 1964, when staff were awarded three weeks' annual holiday. But pension arrangements remained elementary. When John Brown, an engineer at Leven, retired in 1960, he was awarded an *ex-gratia* payment of £150 for long service, 'which sum would also recompense him for the personal tools he had left with us'. A pension scheme was not considered

until the early 1970s. A great improvement to physical working conditions was the installation of heating in the mills at Tayport and Leven in the mid-1960s.

The one change which could have made a significant difference to the efficient management of the business was discounted in 1962. This was the possibility of transferring the whole of the Tayport business to Leven. The opportunity arose because the harbour was still losing money, and its owners, the British Transport Commission, had finally decided to sell it. Donaldson's remained the principal user, and the Commission offered the harbour and ten acres of land to the company for £25,000. In July 1962, the Commission accepted

Donaldson's counteroffer of £5,500. Victor Donaldson felt that the firm's long and patient negotiations had produced 'a good bargain', but he also believed the decision to buy the harbour was 'an act of faith'.

In 1964 the opening of the Forth Road Bridge stimulated the further expansion of the company's sales territories. Work had already begun on the construction of the Tay Road Bridge. Increasing business from new areas such as Edinburgh and the Borders, Oban and Fort William compensated for growing competition in Fife. This was an era when the Scottish market was dominated by as many as thirty principal importers, of which the biggest were firms such as Brownlee, Robinson Dunn, Muirhead, and John Fleming & Company. James Donaldson & Sons Ltd was not yet in the same league.

Major changes were occurring in the trade. More Baltic ports were open longer during the year and the use of drying kilns enabled them to supply seasoned goods even in the early spring. By 1967 the company found that Scandinavian shippers were beginning to use roll-on roll-off ferries to send over lorry loads of timber, which could be delivered directly to the importers' yards or to contractors' building sites. Timber was sent in packages of uniform sizes, usually of one dimension in one length only. The pattern of trade was changing. The growth of major national building contractors led them to use their own timber suppliers rather than those operating in the area where they were working. The largest shippers were taking over well-established agents or setting up their own sales offices in London. Rationalisation and consolidation

A genial portrait of Victor Donaldson in September 1960.

were taking place among the shippers with a trend towards fewer and larger units. In 1966–67, for example, more than 200 smaller shippers from Finland went out of business. This stemmed from the constant desire to curb rising costs and increase economies of scale. The devaluation of sterling in 1967 accelerated the process, when several shippers failed because they had neglected to insure against the appreciation of their own currencies against the pound.

The chairman noted the characteristic pattern of the trade: 'a steady rise in values over a period, producing a heavy stock holding in all the principal importing Countries throughout the world, followed by an easing in values which is usually fairly abrupt'.

In October 1969, Mr Victor, as he was known to his staff, retired from his executive responsibilities after fifty-five years with the company. By now, the firm employed 125 people at Tayport and Leven. Sales had broken the million-pound barrier in the previous year, and record profits of more than £90,000 were achieved in the year of his retirement, a testament to the long working partnership between the Donaldson brothers. Victor remained as chairman of the company until his death on 15 September 1971. His son said that his father had earned the respect of timber agents and staff since both could trust his word: 'He expected enthusiasm to match his own and gave decisions clearly, while always listening to other points of view. When problems arose, he faced up to them squarely and had that clarity of mind which led him to distinguish at once the significant from the trivial.'

'A New Era for the Timber Industry'

6

George Donaldson took over as managing director on his father's retirement in 1969 and became chairman on his father's death in 1971. He took the opportunity to encourage a further move towards centralised management. Consultants advised that administrative departments should be 'reconstructed under individual responsibility' and based at Leven, leaving Tayport as a production unit. This, it was suggested, would achieve better control, increased production and more sales. In the summer of 1970, George Donaldson took charge of production and purchasing, his cousin Colin became sales director and Robert Walker, appointed to the board in April 1970, became responsible for finance and administration. Central departments, one set of books, a joint sales effort and each mill operating as a production unit led to significant trading improvements, particularly at Tayport.

Other changes were made to achieve greater efficiencies. Mechanical accounting systems had been used at Leven since the late 1960s (even with four clerks, the company had rarely been able to keep up to date through the use of manual records). In 1970 the company acquired a heavy-duty front-loading Hyster truck for use at Tayport, freeing up more space for stacking and helping to create a more efficient layout of orders for despatch. As George Donaldson pointed out in 1972, 'A modern timber yard, laid out for fork-truck operation, handling packaged timber, can be operated at substantially lower handling scales than before, and there is no doubt that the introduction of "unitised" ... handling, relatively untried in Scotland until

The discharge of packaged timber from the Tora at Methil around 1980.

a year ago, has had more effect on our costs than most of us anticipated.'

Change at Donaldson's reflected change within the industry. Handling costs fell sharply as cargoes of packaged sawn timber replaced consignments of loose sawn timber. Although packaged timber was first shipped from Sweden to Britain in 1959, the practice was not widely adopted until the early 1970s, following the introduction of drying kilns and the greater use of mechanical handling. Initially, traditional importers were sceptical, believing packaged timber would waste valuable space on board ship, but the shippers responded that ships could be loaded and discharged much more rapidly. Consequently, more voyages could be accomplished more quickly by fewer ships. Gradually, as more importers accepted this innovation, the established practice of making substantial bulk

Reg 'realised above all that success depends on people'

orders declined. Placing smaller orders allowed importers to hold smaller stocks, helping to alleviate the impact of volatile timber prices. For Donaldson's, however, the full benefits of this change remained elusive. Tied to Tayport and Methil for most of its timber imports, the company had to charter vessels whose cargoes were intended entirely for Donaldson's. In larger ports with liner services, one vessel might ship supplies for several importers at a time.

With the death of Victor Donaldson and the retirement of Reg Donaldson from day-to-day business after fifty years, 1971 marked the end of an era. Reg died on 24 September 1974, maintaining until the end an interest in the company despite prolonged illness. The board paid a generous tribute to him: 'he realised above all that success depends on people. He was intensely interested in the lives of all who worked for him – and their families – and there will be many who will recall with love and affection his bountiful generosity in times of trouble.' One indication of the respect with which he was regarded came when he lost his gold signet ring in the snow outside the Tayport mill one wintry evening after a friendly exchange of snowballs with a couple of the tractor men. Realising his loss only after he reached home, he returned to the yard but failed to find the ring. It was almost midnight when there was a knock on his door; the night-watchman had come to tell Reg that he had found the ring.

In the summer of 1971, a serious fire badly damaged the yard at Leven, giving the company the chance to redevelop the site. In consultation with the industry research body, TRADA, plans were drawn up for a new softwood mill at Elm Park, with offices, kiln-drying and hardwood operations on the Wemyss site. New

The Leven Fire

On the night of 16–17 July 1971, a fire broke out at the Leven timber yard. A smouldering stack of timber burst into flames, causing an impressive and dramatic blaze. As one eyewitness recounted, 'At first I could only see the glow and some smoke over the roofs of the houses but even while I was talking to the police the whole thing burst into flames that shot into the sky. The flames were as high as the gas tank across the road. The street was littered with bits of wood and burning ash. It was honestly frightening.' Residents in nearby Riverside Place and Bridge Street snatched their children from their beds and left home to take shelter elsewhere. Sixty firemen, eleven pumps, and engines with a snorkel and a turntable ladder were needed to bring the fire under control, using water from the Leven and the lade close by. Five hundred standards of timber were destroyed, and the mill and offices were seriously damaged. Temporary accommodation was quickly arranged, and production was partially resumed in early August.

offices were opened in Riverside Place in October 1973, followed in early 1976 by the official opening of the new mill at Elm Park by the local MP, Sir John Gilmour. The modern layout made handling timber even easier in the storage areas and production much speedier in the mill, in conjunction with up-to-date machinery.

One unintended consequence of the fire was the postponement of plans already drawn up for substantial improvements at Tayport, although the board had already decided little could be done until the problems caused by the silting up of the harbour entrance had been resolved.

All this was taking place during a period of high inflation, mounting economic uncertainty and industrial disruption. During the dock strike of 1972, for instance, the firm 'had the spectacle of Parana Pine from Brazil unable to discharge at Grangemouth, calling at Brest, Rotterdam and Hamburg on its way to an eventual rendezvous with co-operative stevedores on the Norwegian arctic coast', from where it had to be rechartered to Scotland. In the following year, during the boom stimulated by the government, demand for timber rose 20% and prices soared. The price of Russian white wood, Donaldson's major purchase, rose from £25 per cubic metre in September 1972 to £68 in October 1973. Stock disappeared almost as soon as it was delivered, and sales were based on replacement value, which was almost unheard of. Inevitably, the boom collapsed, but in 1973–74 the company made record profits of half a million pounds on a 20% increase in turnover. This was a generous cushion against falling timber prices as the boom ended. Within a year, merchants were competing

fiercely to sell over-priced stock at uneconomic prices simply to raise cash. Then the pound crashed on international currency markets, accompanied by higher interest rates. In the new era of floating exchange rates, many businesses learned that the art of currency management was as important as shippers' prices. For Donaldson's, although turnover rose steadily in real terms – for this was also a time of high inflation – there was a steep fall in profits during the rest of the 1970s. Nevertheless, compared to some competitors, the company performed much better, thanks partly to its varied customer base. In 1976, George Donaldson set out some of the lessons the company had learned during this tumultuous time: 'To judge the market right becomes the first goal – to price on cost an impossibility. To cultivate relationships to ensure a supply is a necessity, and to remember your friends when times are hard for them is wisdom. To raise your prices while retaining your customers is an art, while finding the funds to fight inflation demands profits.'

Donaldson's directors at the opening of the new offices in Leven in May 1973, showing (left to right) Robert Walker, George Donaldson, Reg Donaldson and Colin Donaldson. One of the rose bowls given by customers in 1910 can be seen on the sideboard filled with dahlias from George Donaldson's garden.

The new Leven mill, opened in 1976, replacing the old one destroyed by fire in 1971.

During the boom, delivery and quality were more important than price for customers, a characteristic still repeated today. Expectations were changing. Instead of holding stocks themselves, customers were buying the timber they needed after they had inspected and selected it at the timber merchant's yard. George Donaldson had a clear view of the future, as he wrote in 1973: 'We are entering a new era for the Timber Industry – an evolution from the role of distributors of a cheap, plentiful raw material into promoters of valuable sophisticated products, manufactured precisely to meet established market needs.' Adding value to timber would be central to the company's future.

Several key steps were taken in this direction. One was selling direct to the public. Colin Donaldson had investigated the idea in 1975, recommending it should be pursued further. It was partly a defensive move intended to stop small customers, who made up a large part of Donaldson's business, drifting away to the retail and wholesale branches already being opened by competitors. The supply chain was changing, with amalgamations and take-overs creating the first of the builder-cum- timber merchant chains. But it was also thought the company would benefit from the separation of smaller customers from larger ones.

The outcome was Donaldson's first direct sales outlet, the Home Improvement Centre. This opened at

Donaldson's first direct sales outlet, the Home Improvement Centre opened in Leven in 1978.

Above left: *In 1983 Donaldson's established a retail outlet in Edinburgh, acquiring J & A Hutton, an old-established merchant, based in Newington Place.*

Left: *Neil Donaldson at Elm Park.*

centre in Airdrie. This moved to premises in Glasgow in 1983, when Donaldson's also acquired J & A Hutton Ltd as a means of opening a retail outlet in Edinburgh.

Colin Donaldson left the business before he could see the success of his idea. In 1977 he applied successfully to train as a minister in the Church of Scotland and towards the end of the year he resigned from the board after twenty-one years with the company.

Another major step was investing in the production of roof trusses, which the directors first discussed in 1976. This idea was promoted enthusiastically by George Donaldson's son Neil. In 1975, when George became president of the Scottish Timber Merchants' & Sawmillers' Association, Neil was the fifth generation of the family to join the company, after completing a course in business studies at Edinburgh Business College. In 1976 he married Valerie Robb and they had three children: Michael, Andrew and Jennifer. After two years at Tayport, Neil spent two years as a salesman before taking a post-graduate business studies diploma at Heriot-Watt University, later adding a master's degree in marketing at the same university in 1983.

Donaldson's had been supplying timber to Scotland's leading timber-framed housebuilders since the early 1970s, establishing excellent customer relationships, which had helped to see the company through the more difficult years of the decade. But making roof trusses had never been seriously considered until a local builder asked the company to make a few trusses for the houses he was erecting. In May 1978 the company decided to open its own roof truss factory, and, in September, George Watson was appointed to run it. Set up with five employees in the former hardwood saw shed, the plant produced thirty-six trusses by the end of November; one year later the

Leven on 7 July 1978 in a converted flooring shed and garage under the management of Arthur Hamilton. It sold sheet materials, ironmongery, doors, insulation material, rainwater goods and kitchen units; offered a 'cut to size' service; and was open for trade and public sales. It was so successful that it was enlarged in 1979 and a garden centre was added in 1981, when it was re-named JD Homecare. A year earlier, Donaldson's had formed a joint venture with W & P Murray Ltd, a home-grown timber firm, to run a second home-improvement company was selling 1,300 trusses every month, and by the early 1980s annual sales were worth £400,000.

George Watson then left the business for a while, and the company struggled to find a capable replacement during a severe economic downturn. Neil Donaldson was convinced that the company could become the dominant suppliers of roof trusses in the Scottish market and his expansion plans persuaded George Watson to return. Factory-made roof trusses had several advantages over trusses put together on site; they were better quality, made from stress-graded timber, less timber was wasted and they could be more rapidly erected on site. By 1985, aiming for a 25% share of the Scottish market, Donaldson's was investing in more sophisticated equipment and looking for larger premises.

George Donaldson was convinced that senior managers should be more involved in shaping the future of the business; he was certain that 'the heart of the problem in maintaining the impetus for a virile industrial enterprise lies more in the calibre and commitment of the executive team than on any other factor'. Like his grandfather, he too believed that senior employees as well as other family members should have a chance to own shares in the company. The company, he felt, would be better served if there was wider ownership of its shares. Firstly, in times of high taxation, there was a risk to the business if a single individual held a substantial majority of the shares; secondly, employees would feel more committed if they had a stake in the business. He transferred many of his own shares to his family, and over the years the number of shareholders expanded to approximately seventy. In 1976 three senior managers, Ron Dickson, Bob Cumming and Archie Honeyman, joined the board and became shareholders. At the

end of 1977, the company recruited for the first time a professional chartered accountant, Alan Sinclair, who became financial controller. He took over as company secretary when Robert Walker retired in 1978 after fifty-one years' service and was appointed a director in 1979.

Despite the difficulties of operating at Tayport, there was some reluctance to confront the situation, mainly for reasons of tradition and sentiment. Problems with the harbour remained intractable. It turned out there was no solution other than regular, costly dredging, which was often carried out unsatisfactorily. Attempts

The offices at Leven, showing technology shifting from the ubiquitous typewriters which will be obsolete within a generation to desktop computers.

This is the visit to Wemyss in the early 1980s of the Czech ambassador Miroslav Houstecky and 1st Secretary Vanicek seen here in photos with (1) Archie Honeyman and (2) Neil Donaldson and Richard Marsh of London agents Price & Pearce.

Above: Sharpening a bandsaw at Elm Park Sawmills.

Above right: Joe Clark, the saw doctor at Elm Park.

Right: Jock Bendix at Elm Park Sawmills.

to increase commercial use of the harbour had met with little success: as well as the problems with silt, the harbour was too small for the bigger vessels being used, and better facilities were offered in Dundee. Given that the modernisation of the Elm Park mill gave the company enough capacity for the time being, there seemed little point in retaining Tayport.

The recession of the late 1970s and early 1980s settled the matter. With falling demand, margins were squeezed repeatedly. It was difficult to reduce stocks quickly enough, prices fell, interest rates rose and the value of the pound plummeted. Although the company escaped with only one small loss throughout this period, the absence of retained profits affected cash flow, prompting the decision in 1982 to scale back operations to reduce borrowing and capital employed. Part of this involved concentrating softwood stocks and sawmilling at Elm Park.

The inevitable logic of all this was ending operations in Tayport. An agreement was reached with local boat owners over the future management of the harbour for leisure purposes; and planning permission was obtained for a mixed development of private housing, sheltered accommodation and small industrial units on most of the surplus land. To progress the development, Donaldson's formed a profitable joint venture with Torwood Homes, a local housebuilder. Ultimately, the purchase made as an act of faith in 1962 turned out to be very valuable. A small depot was maintained at Tayport until the business was transferred in 1990 to new premises in Dundee, ending an involvement with Tayport stretching back 130 years.

As a response to the recession, and as part of a strategy to improve the profitability of the business, three independent divisions – Softwoods, Home Improvement Centre and Timber Engineering – acting as separate profit centres, were created in 1979. This was intended to create greater unity of purpose between the sales, estimating and production functions, improve teamwork, increase opportunities for managers and extend delegation.

Major personnel changes continued to take place. In 1984, Bob Cumming retired after fifty years' service, and, in 1985, Ron Dickson took early retirement after forty-five years with the company. In the same year, the company appointed its first non-executive directors: George R Donaldson (Reg Donaldson's eldest son) and Robin Young, an Edinburgh investment fund manager. It was decided the main board should concentrated on strategy and policy, and day-to-day management would become the responsibility of a new management committee. This was the forerunner of the supervisory and operating boards formed ten years later. The management committee was chaired by Neil Donaldson, who took over as managing director from his father, and included Andy Waddell, George Watson, Robert Stewart, Alan Sinclair and Archie Honeyman.

George Donaldson retained the post of chairman. Handing over the reins for the management of the company to his son broke the pattern of previous generations, where control was surrendered only well past retirement age. It was a lesson his son would remember. George Donaldson had become a widely respected figure within the timber trade. After his presidency of the Scottish Timber Merchants' & Sawmillers' Association from 1975 to 1977, he was president of the Scottish Timber Trade Association from 1978 to 1980, and chaired TRADA, the industry's research and development body, between 1980 and 1982. As he handed over the role of managing director to his son, he accepted the invitation to become the first Scottish merchant to hold office as president of the Timber Trade Federation, an honour Neil would also receive two decades later.

As TTF President, George Donaldson was keen to raise its profile. The cartoon of the annual dinner in 1987 shows how his audience were hoping the TTF would emulate the success of that season's Scottish rugby team.

'Faithful to Wood'

Expansion and Independence 1985–2001

7

Neil had clear ideas about the future. He was fond of quoting Lewis Carroll; when Alice meets the Cheshire Cat in Wonderland, she asks, 'Would you tell me, please, which way I ought to walk from here?' The Cat replies, 'That depends a good deal on where you want to get to.' 'I don't much care where', says Alice. 'Then it doesn't matter which way you walk', responded the Cat. For Neil Donaldson, this encapsulated the importance of knowing where you wanted to go before deciding how to get there. He was influenced by his studies at Heriot-Watt, and it was a report commissioned from Heriot-Watt in 1985 which underlined the importance of setting clear strategic objectives.

One objective was to become Scotland's leading roof truss supplier. The roof truss business needed the freedom to grow under its own identity. On 1 July 1986, Donaldson Timber Engineering Ltd (DTE) was formed under George Watson. Integral to the new company's ambition was the need for larger premises, and with generous regional grants and assistance from the European Union, Donaldson's invested half a million pounds in a new factory, equipped with the most sophisticated computer-controlled plant, at Muiredge, close to Leven.

To improve customer service, DTE set out to deliver the same product at the same price much more quickly. The standard delivery time was twelve weeks, but this varied considerably, creating uncertainty, which was hated by housebuilders. Within six months of moving to Muiredge, DTE was offering guaranteed delivery in seven days. Demand soared and the factory was soon working at capacity. By the late 1980s, DTE accounted

Celebrating 125 Years

On 26 July 1985, James Donaldson & Sons Ltd celebrated 125 years in the timber business. More than 140 guests attended a garden party at Balsusney in Upper Largo, including the Minister for Industry & Education at the Scottish Office, the Lord Lieutenant of Fife, the MP for North East Fife, the Director General of the Timber Trade Federation, the President of RIBA and the Director of TRADA. Bill Donaldson, the second son of Reg Donaldson, and Principal of Newcastle-under-Lyme Grammar School, spoke on behalf of the family, paying tribute to the way in which Neil Donaldson, himself only twenty-nine, was building up a young team of executives for the future.

Roof trusses being made at DTE's Muiredge factory in 2001.

for 15% of Donaldson's turnover, as sales reached £2 million annually; by 1990, the factory was making 5,000 trusses every week and half of Donaldson's profits came from DTE. To achieve this, DTE had introduced 24-hour shift work, and increased the workforce from ten to thirty-five.

While Neil Donaldson adhered to the belief that 'we should always stay faithful to wood', DTE demonstrated how diversification within timber promoted growth. As the chairman, George Donaldson, noted in 1988, Donaldson's had been successful by 'providing a

complete service, adding value through processing activities, rather than competing with low-cost merchanting operations'. Reliance upon softwoods dropped from more than 90% of turnover at the start of the decade to 50% by the end. Turnover grew from £5.5 million in 1980 to more than £21 million in 1990, while

The Homecare branch at the Wemyss sawmill. Ronnie, the driver, was still working for Robert Summers Transport in 2021.

Right: Neil Donaldson with Keith Graham and an unknown visitor at Methil Docks with timber imported from Honkilahti in Finland.

Below: Neil Donaldson with operations director George Watson at the opening of the company's new timber treatment plant in 1990.

operating profits more than doubled in real terms from £320,000 to £1.3 million.

In 1990, the James Donaldson Group was structured around four divisions: DTE, JD Homecare, Timber, and Central Services. In 1989–90, JD Homecare moved its retail and wholesale depots in Glasgow and Edinburgh to better premises and opened a new depot in Dundee, taking over from Tayport. Elm Park concentrated on supplying the Group's biggest customers, increasing throughput from 20,000 cubic metres in 1978 to 70,000 in 1990, most of it still shipped through Methil.

More timber was being imported from Canada, since it was cheaper than timber from Scandinavia and the Baltic, where production costs were rising, exchange rates were unfavourable, and output was suffering disruption from the collapse of Communism. The company had always been a pioneer in treating timber to preserve it, acquiring its first treatment plant from Hickson's of Castleford in the early 1960s; and as demand for this service increased, especially from DTE, £250,000 was invested in a larger plant, which was installed in 1990.

Donaldson's performed better than its rivals during the 1980s as many family businesses disappeared from the Scottish timber trade. Some vanished forever, while others were swallowed up by larger national companies, a pattern repeated at regular intervals during the next few decades. Through this process and through its own successful growth, Donaldson's joined the premier league of Scottish timber companies. Shareholders were proud of the firm's history and constant in their support of the company's independence. Some years later, George Donaldson summed this up, saying that 'a business like ours with its five generations of history and intense family loyalty is directed to the future, not the nearest exit'. But, he added, the company must 'strive for excellence in performance, so that a more liberal dividend policy could be pursued, now that the shareholding circle was widening'. It was important not only to run the business in trust for the shareholders but also to strengthen links with them as their numbers grew. In 1989, for instance, it was agreed all shareholders should receive the minutes of the Annual General Meeting. In 1991, when a record number of shareholders, particularly from the younger generation, attended the event, it was also agreed that the directors would hold briefings for shareholders during the year. This was appreciated by shareholders

as another recession made life difficult for the business in the early 1990s. They were reassured by what one shareholder, Bill Donaldson, called 'the conscientious manner in which shareholders were regularly informed on the company's progress'.

Following a small loss in 1992–93, the Group reduced borrowings, cut costs and exercised greater credit control. DTE's positive cash flow was a great advantage. DTE was still growing and seemed immune from the impact of the recession, which put several rivals out of business.

The company lost two senior managers in the early 1990s. Ian Johnson retired early in 1992 after forty-seven years with Donaldson's. Archie Honeyman, who was responsible for running Elm Park, died suddenly in March 1992. A knowledgeable man, tough, abrasive and forthright, he was recognised as 'one of the most effective traders in Scotland and had applied his skills with absolute loyalty to Donaldson's'.

By this time, DTE had secured a third of the Scottish roof truss market and was looking at opportunities in England. This was in line with Neil Donaldson's vision of replicating in the much larger English market operations that had been successful in Scotland. Although timber-framed housing accounted for only 4% of the English market, this was worth two and a half times the value of the Scottish market. Moving cautiously, DTE established a small unit on a greenfield site in Cramlington in Northumberland, close enough to Muiredge for effective management. The site began making trusses in May 1992. With its outstanding delivery record in Scotland, the new outpost quickly made inroads in the English market, where service was generally poor. In 1995, DTE took over a competitor, F J Reeves, based on a 7-acre site in Ilkeston in Derbyshire. As Donaldson Timber Engineering (Midlands), the plant was modernised, and the culture was transformed under new ownership, with greater delegation and responsibility for managers and the participation of employees in profit-sharing.

By now, DTE was turning over £15 million and making 8,500 trusses every week. Further acquisitions followed in England, including Oxford Timber Components in 1999, while a new facility was developed at Ashford in Kent in 2000 and a sixth factory at Andover on the south coast in 2001.

Elm Park performed badly in the first half of the 1990s. Although action was taken (including investment in computerised stock control) to remedy unsatisfactory practices, performance did not improve materially until Scott Cairns was appointed to run the site in 1996. In his late twenties, Scott Cairns already had considerable experience of the timber trade from his previous employment with Mallinson's in Grangemouth. To revive Elm Park's fortunes, he made a series of radical changes. Building on the nucleus of a good team among existing staff, he made a number of external appointments, gave

managers greater responsibility and encouraged senior staff to exchange views by meeting regularly every week. The theme of improved communications was extended to the rest of the workforce with a more frequent exchange of information, underpinned by Scott Cairns' open-door policy.

The 12-acre site was transformed by landscaping, properly laid-out car parking, new offices and improved hygiene facilities. The old aerodrome hangar was demolished, replaced by a new timber storage shed. Most of the mill plant was superseded

In September 2000, Henry McLeish, the local MP and MSP, and later briefly First Minister, seen here with Scott Cairns and Neil Donaldson, opened JDT's new Elm Park facilities, also depicted here.

The open plan office at Elm Park in 2001, computers having replaced typewriters.

The Leven sawmill and yard in 1997.

by technologically advanced equipment capable of producing a wide range of components and adding value to a basic material product.

Links with long-standing suppliers, based on good personal relationships, were developed to ensure the consistent quality of the timber delivered to Donaldson's. An aggressive sales campaign revived the business's customer base.

Given the critical importance of delivery times, handling and logistics were improved, allowing Donaldson's to offer customers delivery within forty-eight hours. Stock controls were overhauled, and stock holdings reduced to six or seven weeks at any one time.

In 1998 the timber business was given its own identity as James Donaldson Timber Ltd (JDT). Over the following three years JDT returned much better results, above the industry average, with the volume of timber handled rising from 70,000 cubic metres to 110,000 cubic metres.

The funding of the growth of DTE and JDT was helped by the proceeds from the sale of two investments in the late 1990s. Firstly, the Wemyss site in Leven was sold to Sainsbury's for £2.5 million, the culmination of a process that had begun when the supermarket first expressed an interest in the site in 1985. The area was zoned for retail development in 1992, but it still took

The Boards

The supervisory board included non-executive directors as well as family members. The valuable contributions made by George R Donaldson and Robin Young were continued by their successors, Colin Rutherford and Randolph Murray. Murray, who had recently retired as managing director of Torwood Timber Engineering, was well known to the family and sympathetic to the company's ethos and culture. Neil Donaldson had known Colin Rutherford for several years. An able chartered accountant, Rutherford had established his own consultancy following the sale of the practice he had founded to one of the major accountancy firms. The first operating board comprised Neil Donaldson, George Watson, Scott Cairns, Alan Sinclair, Ian Hawkins, Callum Henderson and Simon White. They all participated in an executive share-incentive scheme based on the attainment of stringent financial targets.

five years before a deal was concluded. Donaldson's transferred its head office to a suite in the old Haig office block in Markinch, while Sainsbury's built new premises for Donaldson's on the Leven site. Initially intended for JD Homecare, the premises were let to a third party in 1998. Secondly, the Group sold its interest in an expanded merchanting business, Firstbase Timber, into which JD Homecare had been merged, to the national merchant Wolseley Centres plc. Recognising the need to fund future investment, the Group established a modest investment portfolio, including a 50% stake in an established hardwood importer in Oxfordshire, a stake in an Estonian sawmill and interests in a variety of unit and investment trusts.

By the end of the twentieth century, the James Donaldson Group had sales of nearly £36 million, operating profits of nearly £1.5 million, and employed 350 people. The Group was one of Scotland's leading timber companies and, through DTE, a major force in UK roof truss manufacturing. While remaining an independent family-owned business, the Group recognised the critical importance of employing talented professional managers, culminating in the creation of supervisory and operating boards in 1997. This, George Donaldson suggested,

married the traditions of a family business with the demands of the professional world of competition.

In the summer of 2001, George Donaldson stepped down from the chairmanship of the Group after thirty years, having started the process of transforming Donaldson's from a family-owned and family-run timber merchant into a family-owned and professionally managed timber business. He had always believed that the family culture and status of the Group, with its emphasis upon people, gave Donaldson's the resilience needed to endure in the modern timber industry. He had outlined his continuing ambition for the business at the company's Annual General Meeting in 1996: 'It is my belief that our paramount goal in Donaldson's is to retain our independence as a proud family-controlled business free of institutional investment, while building on our reputation as a significant force in the industry.' His contribution to the UK timber industry was recognised by the award of the CBE in the summer of 2000. His son Neil would follow his father's example both within the Group and outside it and had already been chairman of TRADA. With George Donaldson's retirement, Neil was now completely responsible for the future direction of the business.

'At the Forefront of Our Industry'

A New Millennium, A New Generation 2001–

8

The story of James Donaldson & Sons over the next two decades falls neatly into two halves – the first ten years or so before the world recession, and the years immediately afterwards. The Group has overcome considerable external challenges. While the timber industry's trading cycle was still one of peaks and troughs, the recession was the most severe global economic downturn since the 1930s. On top of this came the disruption to traditional supply patterns as Scandinavian suppliers found it financially more rewarding to send more timber to other parts of the world. In the UK, the pace of consolidation accelerated as private equity funds acquired several long-established businesses. On the other hand, this incursion indicated confidence in the industry's future, based on the long-term national need for more housing,

and timber's position as the most sustainable of building materials. Most recently, and perhaps most acutely of all, the Group had to surmount the crisis created by the COVID-19 pandemic.

In meeting all these challenges, the Group has emerged stronger. Before the world recession, turnover and operating profits doubled in real terms; after the recession, the Group achieved an almost unbroken run of record sales and profits, while during the pandemic the Group quickly recouped its initial losses, and parts of the business achieved record results. While most of this growth has been organic, the Group has added new sites and businesses, some more successful than others, extending its coverage of the UK. Learning how to manage a bigger, more complex business has been a constant challenge, and the central service support given

to group businesses in areas such as human resources, marketing and technology has expanded significantly.

Neil Donaldson stepped down as group managing director in 2011, handing over to Scott Cairns, the first person from outside the family to hold the position. At the same time, Michael Donaldson, known as Mike, and Andrew Donaldson, known as Andy, the sixth generation of the family, became actively involved, paving the way for them to take over as chairman and managing director. The supervisory board was refreshed by the appointment of new non-executive directors, and the Group invested in developing internal management talent while recognising the value of recruiting externally when necessary.

In 2001 the Group made one of its most important acquisitions, buying MGM Timber (Scotland) Ltd. Founded in 1982 by Joe McConville and Charlie McLeish, Perth-based MGM was an important customer of JDT. It was the latter's managing director, Scott Cairns, who recognised MGM's potential. It offered the chance to develop a completely new outlet for JDT's products and dilute the growing purchasing power and influence of the national merchants who were already eyeing up the business. It took some time for the supervisory board to agree to make an offer for MGM. They remembered the unsuccessful experiment with Firstbase and worried that existing merchant customers might resent the Group's acquisition of a competing business. 'There was', recalled Scott Cairns, 'quite some debate for quite some time.' Eventually, however, the board gave the go-ahead, and James Donaldson bought half of MGM, although this was done through a subsidiary to minimise any antagonism from customers.

At the time of the deal, MGM had six branches and annual sales of £11 million. More branches were opened, but profitability was fragile. The Group was frustrated by its inability to exercise any decisive influence on the business because of the 50:50 joint venture agreement with MGM's founders. This provided for the Group to buy out the founders after three years; to try and break the deadlock, Scott Cairns and Neil Donaldson proposed buying them out a year early. Members of the supervisory board were concerned that the price being asked was much too high. 'There was', Scott Cairns recalled, 'great division between everyone; there was suspicion, fear – there were objections.' Given the scale of the investment involved, it was, Alan Sinclair confessed, 'the toughest of decisions'. But with Scott Cairns and Neil Donaldson strongly in favour, the supervisory board agreed to proceed. Scott Cairns' enthusiasm was crucial in persuading the board. Feeling he had gone as far as he could in managing JDT, he was eager for a new challenge. The outright takeover of the business, which in aggregate cost almost £6 million, was completed on 1 April 2005, and in the Group review that year Neil Donaldson stressed: 'we are convinced that the strategy of vertical integration is correct'.

Scott Cairns became MGM's managing director. With ten branches – Perth, Dundee, Grangemouth, Dunfermline, Glasgow, Glenrothes, Hillington, Wishaw, Edinburgh and Inverness – MGM had sales of £16 million but was still losing money. Scott Cairns applied the same ethos, team spirit, customer focus and flexibility that had been so successful at JDT. Under his enthusiastic leadership, hands-on approach and involvement in detail, MGM became Scotland's leading independent merchant chain by focusing not just on price but on every aspect of customer service. He worked closely with the financial director, David Mansell, and the sales director, Brian Smith, and within

a year they had returned MGM to profit. A business development director, Grant Wilson, was recruited in 2007, and in 2008 two more branches, in Prestwick and Oban, were opened. In that year the business recorded operating profits of a million pounds on turnover of £30 million; MGM accounted for almost a third of Group turnover and more than a quarter of the Group's operating profit, more than justifying the decision to invest in the business.

The MGM joint venture was one of several in which the Group took part during the first decade of the new century; none was satisfactory, dissuading the Group from participating in any more. Attempts to repeat the success of the partnership with Torwood Homes came to nothing; an investment in an Estonian sawmill lost money; and DTE's joint venture in Eire ended with the collapse of the Irish housing market.

One of the Group's investments was as equal partners in a hardwood business, Parker Kislingbury, based at Brill in Buckinghamshire, in 2001. This joint venture was equally frustrating: as the business ran into difficulties, the Group was unable to take decisive action. Eventually, in 2006, the other partner sold his stake to the Group; a new managing director was appointed; margins improved and the business remained profitable as the world recession began.

When Scott Cairns left JDT, Iain Torrance succeeded him as managing director. By then, JDT was making sales of £18 million with operating profits of more than £800,000. The business was well regarded throughout the industry, receiving the accolade of Supplier of the Year from the Scottish Independent Merchants Buying Association in 2002. In the same year, JDT became the first timber business in Scotland and the second in the UK to achieve accreditation for the Forest Stewardship Council, following this in 2003 with accreditation from the Pan European Forestry Council.

Scott had identified Iain as an ideal candidate to take over from him, and Iain was receptive: he was looking for a new challenge after sixteen years with JDT's main rival, International Timber, where he was sales director. In fact, he had just secured the contract to supply the National Buying Group, a contract previously held by JDT. Iain took up his post at JDT in April 2006 – and by the end of the year JDT had won back the National Buying Group contract.

He quickly settled into his new role. As he reflected later, Donaldson's 'is still very much a family business – you feel like you belong'. He found the autonomy given to senior managers refreshing, relishing the fact that 'our destiny is in our own hands', and felt that the close-knit team and flat management structure allowed the business to be very responsive to customers and suppliers. Torrance was impressed with the workforce – 'that's what makes the business tick' – and the development of Elm Park, which had become one of the most modern operations of its type in the industry. He was determined to make sure it remained that way.

Building on Scott Cairns' achievements, Iain Torrance encouraged managers to use their initiative. He and his team added more customers, and for the first time JDT began supplying major state organisations, such as local councils and the Scottish prison service. With an expanding product range, sales increased by 7% over four years. The relationship between JDT and MGM blossomed, benefiting both businesses. As supplies became scarcer and prices soared, JDT fostered existing highly valued long-

standing relationships with key suppliers in Scandinavia, particularly Finland and Sweden. By 2008, in the face of fierce competition, turnover had risen to £29 million, with a further rise in profits, as JDT handled twice as much timber as its nearest rival.

This was a boom time in the trade, yet the one company struggling within the Group was the market leader in its field. By 2002, DTE was the UK's largest truss manufacturer, with a market share of 13%. The business appeared to be on an upwards trajectory: as well as the new factory in Ireland, another was opened in Ipswich, and the Buckhaven plant benefited from investment in more efficient equipment. In 2004, DTE was the first roof truss producer to gain accreditation from the Pan European Forestry Council.

Yet DTE began to fall behind other parts of the Group. The Ilkeston sawmill shut down in 2006; the Ipswich factory never made money (it was eventually closed in 2009); and the performance of other branches was lacklustre. George Watson's leadership came into question as it was clear DTE's management was overstretched by the company's growth across the UK. As the supervisory board later observed, 'the DTE business had … been run into the ground and the cracks papered over'. Rather than confront these problems, however, George Watson was still pressing ahead with expansion plans, and it was the supervisory board who decided to remedy the situation, appointing Jeremy English in 2007 to run all DTE's sites south of the border other than Cramlington. This proved unacceptable to George Watson, who left on 31 March 2008 after thirty years with the Group.

By then, recession was looming. The signs were there with the bursting of the Irish housing bubble, which put paid to DTE's Irish joint venture in 2007. Another indication was the collapse of DTE's biggest competitor, Palgrave Brown, which went into administration in November 2008. Ironically, this gave JDT the opportunity it had been seeking to enter a completely new sector. Under Iain Torrance, JDT was pushing into the English market, with the idea of repeating in England those activities operating successfully in Scotland. As with DTE, JDT began developing sales in the north-east of England, given its proximity and population, before looking to the north-west, a market with a population larger than Scotland's.

Under the name Alfred Hulme, Palgrave Brown operated a site at Chorley in Lancashire. The Group had previously considered buying the business before it began expanding rapidly during the boom, securing a 14% share of the UK truss market. Like DTE, Palgrave Brown grew too quickly, and its failure gave the Group the chance to take over the entire business. Bearing in mind the lessons of DTE, the Group rejected this opportunity, but instead acquired the Chorley site, mainly because it gave Donaldson's the opportunity to move into the MDF market: Chorley was one of only five UK sites making primed white MDF mouldings. This, it was felt, outweighed the

physical limitations of the site, which was spread over various levels, making production costly and inefficient. Even so, within a year of James Donaldson & Sons taking it over in 2008, and despite the recession, the site was breaking even.

Although the Group remained profitable, its results for the year ending 31 March 2009 were scarred by the impact of what Neil Donaldson described as 'the most severe correction to the housing market in my lifetime … we have had to adapt our ways'. One major customer, Persimmon, cut its predicted output for the year from 16,000 units to 11,000. Turnover fell from £97 million to £78 million, operating profits from £3.6 million to £1 million, and pre-tax profits from £3 million to £700,000. The Group's borrowings had fallen sharply since buying MGM, and gearing was relatively low, but finance director Ian Hawkins, who had taken over from Alan Sinclair in 2001, found the banks difficult to deal with. Credit insurance became impossible to obtain: when cover was withdrawn from one major housebuilding customer, creating a potential liability of £750,000, the Group had to manage the risk itself. Neil Donaldson's decision to build up an investment portfolio as an easily realisable reserve of last resort came into its own, giving the Group invaluable temporary funding of half a million pounds for the purchase of timber at the end of 2009 in advance of major price rises. Although the Group was initially hesitant in cutting costs, every effort was made to reduce spending, manage credit more intensively, husband cash more effectively and protect margins rather than pursue turnover. It was, said Neil Donaldson, 'a desperate time', but the business was 'brutal' in cutting costs, 'and we never lost sight of our customers, customer service and the need to keep looking for

The Next Generation

Mike and Andy Donaldson both wanted to take time to gain a deep understanding of the business and absorb the accumulated knowledge and experience of their father and other senior colleagues.

Mike had wanted to be part of the family firm ever since he had taken a summer job in the business. He spent a year at JDT before joining DTE in 2006, where he was involved with the development of the Structural Insulated Roofing System, which won NHBC accreditation in 2007. In that year, he was the first MSc graduate in Timber Industrial Management at the Napier University Centre for Timber Engineering. In November 2008, as the recession began to bite, he was running DTE's Scottish operations, based at Buckhaven, where the number of employees more than halved within a year. It was, he recalled, a challenging time. He then joined JDT, working in sales management, and it was while he was with JDT that he joined the supervisory board in 2014. He became commercial director of MGM and in 2018 was appointed deputy chairman of the group. When his father, Neil, stepped down in 2020, Mike succeeded him as group chairman. Mike and his wife, Sarah, have three children: Molly, Archie and Freddie, part of the seventh generation of the Donaldson family.

Andrew decided he wanted experience of the business world outside the Group before deciding whether to join. After graduating in Management Studies at Aberdeen University, he qualified as a chartered accountant with KPMG, where he spent more than four years. There he met his wife, Alyson, and they would later have two children, Arran and Ava. When Andy joined the Group in the summer of 2010, his aim was to ensure he gained experience of the business outside the finance department. In the following year, he was made MGM's commercial director, helping the management team in a business that was thriving in the face of the recession. At his request, he spent more than a year as the sales representative for MGM's Broxburn branch before moving to JDT, tackling the challenges presented by the sites at Brill and Chorley. He joined the supervisory board in 2015, and in 2018 he succeeded Ian Hawkins as group finance director. Two years later he took over from Scott Cairns as chief executive officer.

opportunities'. A good management team 'and a determination not to be derailed' helped the Group to say in profit, even increasing dividends. The supervisory board was constantly challenging senior management, insisting several initiatives should be deferred, including a long overdue move to new offices. By 2011, turnover had returned to pre-recession levels, and trading and pre-tax profits exceeded £2 million.

By then, significant changes affecting the future of the business were underway. Neil Donaldson, whose respect in the industry had been reflected in his election as president of the Timber Trade Federation in 2006, was looking towards the time when he would step down from the business. He hoped that eventually his two sons would take the helm. Mike had been with the business since 2005; and his brother, since 2010. They were still young men, Mike 31 years old, Andy 29 years old in 2011.

The gap between the generations was filled by Scott Cairns, who was appointed group managing director in the spring of 2011. Scott was ready for the challenge of his new position. 'I asked to do it, I wanted to do it, I sought it out.' The business was still coping with the economic downturn. Turnover was rising, partly because of market forces, with shortages forcing up the price of timber, but margins were still under pressure, and this would remain the trend for the next few years. Shortly after Scott's appointment, Neil Donaldson, who remained executive chairman, told shareholders that 'there is a really genuine desire for everyone in the business not to let this recession and slump in housebuilding affect us. We are all, under Scott's leadership, looking for greater efficiencies and more focus.'

Given a broad remit, Scott Cairns worked closely with Neil Donaldson, meeting weekly, discussing every material issue. It was not an easy time to take over. The next couple of years, Scott confessed, were probably the most difficult he had ever faced in his career. Reporting to shareholders in 2012–13, he described the year as unquestionably the most challenging of his career, with little activity in housebuilding or general construction, low selling prices, extreme competition and terrible weather. Scott applied to the Group the same approach that had been successful at MGM, which was based on an unwavering focus on the customer. He had the advantage of working with a well-established senior management team he knew well, and he fostered closer collaboration between companies to make the most of the benefits available from working

Scott Cairns.

together as a group. Costs were constantly scrutinised and an ambitious rolling 3-year plan concentrated minds on financial targets, while making sure the Group remained nimble enough to adapt if targets were thrown off course by the markets.

MGM, where David Mansell took over as managing director, was the only business to remain significantly profitable during the downturn. In the recession, MGM carried on recruiting new people, helping to win more customers and boost performance. Not a single redundancy was made. The business changed its kitchen supplier, opting for a leading German manufacturer. Instead of trying to promote kitchens in every branch, where there was often limited space, inhibiting sales, this time efforts were concentrated on Edinburgh, one of the bigger branches. The improved display helped sales, complemented by knowledgeable staff and capable designers. Over the next few years, the concept would be extended successfully to other branches when more space became available. A new branch was acquired in Broxburn in 2010, returning a profit within its first year, contributing to record sales and profits. With costs under control, branch performance improving – the loss-making Oban branch was sold in 2013 – and a widening product range, this trend continued. One of these new products was insulation, alongside the kitchen units, building membranes and laminated panels. In 2012, James Donaldson Insulation was started under the MGM umbrella. MGM took advantage of the expertise of a team who had left another insulation business after it had been taken over. The attraction was to bring the margin earned by the distributor into the Group. Getting the new business going was not easy since it had no credit rating, and its suppliers were under pressure from national competitors not to deal with it. Nevertheless, the reputation of the management team was a definite advantage, and the business, based in Coatbridge, made an impact on the Scottish construction industry.

DTE was seriously affected by the recession, which exposed its over-reliance on housing, and the business had to lose 150 jobs. It also highlighted the weakness of restructuring DTE into two divisions, north and south, under separate leadership, which failed to deliver the undivided focus on customers, sales and service needed in challenging times. Neil Donaldson temporarily took over the business, recruiting two able directors to help turn it around. Jonathan Fellingham became operations director; and Avi Basu, finance director. Concentrating on sales, Neil began bringing DTE's culture into line with that of the rest of the Group. In December 2009, Jonathan Fellingham was appointed managing director. Like Iain Torrance, Jonathan liked the open, honest, friendly culture, based on family values, with transparent and free-flowing communication. In turn, he invited Callum Henderson to fill his previous position, based on Callum's knowledge of DTE as head of HR. At Buckhaven, where the workforce was much smaller, changes included a better canteen, better washrooms, and a bonus system based on quality rather than volume. Employees began working as a team instead of focusing on individual performance. Greater co-operation was encouraged between the design team and the sales team. Effective sales management and quality training schemes were set up, and weekly management meetings were introduced. The response of the workforce was excellent, appreciating the improvements being made and the chance for greater participation. Subsequently, similar changes were made under Callum Henderson at Ilkeston.

Under Jonathan Fellingham and his team, DTE developed a new strategy: targeting volume housebuilders to raise output; fostering co-operation rather than competition between DTE's branches; and concentrating joist manufacturing on one site, Ilkeston, which had better management, a better location and greater capacity. This was backed by integrating systems across the company and moving to a more effective financial software package. The recession boosted the joist business since several companies gave up their production, creating room in the market for DTE.

Increasing output as a result helped DTE to maximise economies of scale and increase profitability. Similarly, while many businesses were reducing jobs, DTE carried on recruiting, training a pool of talent on which housebuilders came to depend as they cut back on their own in-house technical expertise. In this way, and by building up long-term relationships with customers, DTE established a reputation as a trusted supplier. Under general manager Luke Roberts, Ilkeston had made DTE the biggest manufacturer of Posi Joists and the largest distributor of engineered I-Beams in the UK. By 2012, DTE was the Group's most profitable business.

For JDT, the recession was, said Iain Torrance, 'a horrible time'. Although the business remained marginally profitable, turnover slumped by 40% and jobs had to go. Chorley remained a difficult site to manage, Scott Cairns describing it in 2015 as 'organised chaos'. For too long, its problems were compounded by operating three different businesses – MDF, joists and timber – reporting to three different managements. Transferring joist production to Ilkeston was the right decision for the Group but it reduced Chorley's turnover, making profitability more difficult to achieve. JDT did benefit from Chorley's MDF activities, the original reason for buying the business. There was plenty of potential nationwide for JDT in white primed MDF, a fragmented market characterised by small, overcommitted and underinvested businesses. JDT invested in new plant and equipment for MDF production, which helped JDT to become the first exporting business in the Group as well as making it the leading supplier of primed MDF in Scotland.

JDT also became responsible for another challenging operation, Parker Kislingbury at Brill, from 2013. It turned out that too much faith had been placed in previous management. Standards of service declined and the business lost its way, losing its reputation for quickly turning around work that rivals could not take on. The Group tried to resolve the situation, Randolph Murray and Alan Sinclair making such regular visits to the site that they became known as 'the M&S recovery team'. When the business was rebranded as part of JDT, Iain Torrance was assisted by Andy Donaldson, who was also involved with the Chorley site. Softwood was added to Brill's niche hardwood business, but the two businesses did not mix well. The Group persevered for too long with Brill, eventually closing it in 2015. Staff remained committed to the business until the very last day, when Andy Donaldson locked the padlocks on the gate of the leasehold site. The plant and equipment were moved for handling hardwood at Elm Park at Leven, where a hardwood specialist was later appointed. Elm Park itself, where Mike Donaldson was for a time part of the management team, was still making money, although margins were under pressure, and JDT was achieving a record share of the Scottish market.

All the work put in by management and employees around the Group paid off. In 2014–15, Group turnover rose to a record £132 million but, more importantly, operating profits increased from £2.8 million to a record £4.8 million. It was, said Neil Donaldson, 'a stellar year for the business'. The Group emerged from the downturn stronger than ever by responding to changing priorities among customers, concerned as much about quality, service and delivery as price. As a result, the Group secured its relationship with the emerging national buying chains. Moreover, the Group also succeeded in allaying anxieties among merchants

Corrie McPherson, HR Advisor, with Mandy Cooper, HR Manager, in the background, in the Glenrothes offices. (McAteer)

Donaldson House, Glenrothes, the company's purpose-built head office, opened in 2016. (McAteer)

Carolyn Shields, Group Financial Controller, in the Glenrothes offices. (McAteer)

about its ownership of MGM. A return to more prosperous times made it possible to revive the project for new head offices. Planning permission was given for a site acquired in Glenrothes in 2014, and work began the following year, funded partly by proceeds from the Group's successful investment portfolio. The building was completed in 2016. Over the next few years, the Group achieved a series of record results. As well as rising sales and profits, earnings per share, 25p in 2010–11, reached 113p in 2018–19, while the number of full-time employees exceeded 800, an increase of 70% on the number employed prior to the recession. At the Group's 100th AGM in 2019, Neil Donaldson could say, 'Your business is now at the forefront of our industry. Competitors are trying to emulate us.' As Scott Cairns observed, given challenging external factors, ranging from the anxiety about Brexit to the impact on timber supplies after the imposition US tariffs on Canadian lumber, 'to perform so well in a period of constant macro uncertainty is no mean feat'.

Every company in the Group played its part in this success. JDT cemented its relationship with housebuilders, reducing its customer base to guarantee supplies. Personal relationships, said Iain Torrance, still matter in the timber trade, and most relationships with suppliers and customers are personal and long term. 'We try to look after them well.' JDT capitalised on its position in the MDF market in 2016, making the Group's biggest single capital investment, worth £1.7 million, in a state-of-the-art automated MDF moulding, painting and packaging line at Elm Park. Today, with annual sales of more than £6 million, MDF makes up 17% of Elm Park's

Elm Park – Quick-set Powermat Weinig moulder. (McAteer)

Elm Park: high-speed Weinig H23A softwood moulder. (McAteer)

Elm Park: production of machined softwood. (McAteer)

Elm Park: MDF moulding and quality checks. (McAteer)

Elm Park: a stack of whitewood flooring. (McAteer)

turnover, making an important contribution to JDT's strategy of increasing value-added products, over which the business has greater control than the traditionally volatile timber market. JDT has built on its position as the largest business of its type in Scotland by sending products to Northern Ireland and south of the border as far as Scarborough, but it is in England that the focus for future growth lies. Resolving the difficulties involved in the management of the Chorley site is essential since JDT's ambitions in the English market rest in large part on expanding the MDF business.

England must also be the next port of call for MGM, whose Scottish business is mature. A couple of branches have been added in recent years, one in Hamilton and another in Edinburgh. Further growth in Scotland has come from enlarging existing branches: Paisley, for instance, covers 15,000 square feet, Glasgow 20,000 square feet and Inverness 10,000 square feet. Another avenue is ecommerce, and the expectation is that customers will be able to buy online from the end of 2020. In 2016 by acquiring Nu Style, an Aberdeen-based manufacturer of shower panels, toilet cubicles and hygiene units, seeking capital investment for expansion, MGM has enhanced its margins by eliminating the need to buy through a distributor and has improved its ability to supply products to

MGM: Clydebank branch.

Right: MGM: Edinburgh City branch.

Below right: MGM: Paisley branch.

Bottom: MGM: Glenrothes branch.

major customers, for example local authorities. Nu Style products – the business is widening its range through the development of products, for example an interlocking panel – are being marketed to MGM's existing customers.

DTE had achieved the greatest success in the much bigger English market and renewed its ambition to expand as the UK economy improved. In 2016, on the back of outstanding results, the chairman highlighted DTE's 'great market share, exceptional customer satisfaction ratings and a commercially savvy team with growing experience'. In 2015 a site had been opened in Warrington to cover the north-west, and in 2018 a roof truss business in Cambridge was acquired to cover East Anglia. DTE had limited success in developing new products, partly because these could be copied

easily and cheaply by competitors, and instead built on its technical expertise, offering advice to builders on techniques for erecting roofs. In 2019, Luke Roberts, who had been an outstanding general manager, succeeded Jonathan Fellingham as managing director.

In 2018–19 the Group's sales exceeded £182 million, and profits were more than £8.6 million. The business was substantially larger than a decade previously. It had outperformed rivals by cultivating close working relationships with customers, responding to their needs, offering better service and better-quality products. Its success made it attractive to private equity funds whose investment was driving the consolidation of the market, and the Group turned down a serious approach from one investor. There was some anxiety that private equity would threaten the Group's position but this proved unfounded. Instead, the presence of private equity has been positive for Donaldson's. Firstly, the very fact of their investment is a vote of confidence in the future of the UK timber industry. Secondly, customers value the Group as an independent family business, taking a long-term view, compared with the short-term horizons of private equity investors. Thirdly, the Group has been able to recruit several talented managers dissatisfied with the management approach taken by some of those investors.

The Group's ambition was evident, as part of the Group's strategy of investing in added-value timber related products, in the acquisition of two businesses from Rowan Timber in early 2020: Rowan Manufacturing, based in Plains, which made door sets; and Smith & Frater, based in Grangemouth, which produced kitchen carcasses. These acquisitions added £20 million in turnover and more than a hundred employees.

> *'We will attract the very best people for the long-term future of the business'*

As more people joined the business, which now had nearly a thousand employees, overtly promoting the Group's values became increasingly important. In 2010, George Donaldson, proposing the vote of thanks at the AGM, had spoken about the qualities that had sustained the business for so long. He highlighted the importance of nurturing people and fostering teamwork, mentioning by name David Seath and Ronnie Garrett as examples of those who had developed their potential. Ten years later, they were still with the business, David as JDT's sales manager, Ronnie as one of MGM's senior branch managers, belonging to a pool of people who have spent most of their working lives with Donaldson's. One consultant, recalled Neil Donaldson, was amazed to discover that the ten people he asked to meet had an aggregate service with Donaldson's totalling 180 years. 'We have continued to invest to make James Donaldson & Sons a place people want to come to work', Mike Donaldson told shareholders in 2018. 'We will attract the very best people for the long-term future of the business.'

Recognising the importance of sustaining these values, Scott Cairns had led an exercise to formally encapsulate the Group's culture for the first time. Out of this emerged the mission, vision and values, which were rolled out across every business in 2016.

Mission

A family of companies delivering value through innovation in timber to customers, employees and local communities since 1860.

Vision

Ambitious, Innovative, Respected – The outstanding independent national supplier to the construction industry.

Values

- We put customers, service and quality at the core of everything we do
- We conduct our business with absolute integrity
- We empower our people with opportunities in a safe workplace
- We deliver sustainable financial and environmental performance
- We embrace our future through our proud family legacy

The impact was overwhelmingly positive. Annual employee surveys were initiated, leading to several innovations in the workplace, from quarterly works council meetings and a new works bonus scheme to investment in better canteens and toilets. A company magazine was introduced to keep people more closely in touch with what was going on.

The regular visits made by the chairman to every part of the business were important for encouraging cultural change, retaining staff and sustaining morale. Neil Donaldson had been struck by the comment of a friend, who confessed that the first time he had met his own managing director was when he received a long-service award. He was determined no one should say the same thing about Donaldson's. He visited every site twice a year, making himself available to any member of staff as part of his belief that every employee should be treated fairly, a practice continued by Scott Cairns and Mike Donaldson. Directors of the different subsidiaries have taken a greater personal interest in the sites under their management, leading by example, showing rather than telling. It has been, suggested Callum Henderson, about connecting people, being inclusive, taking time, being persistently persuasive, an approach that reaps rewards in the long term.

With eight separate companies, there was also a need for the Group to become more professional. This resulted in a series of key appointments in recent years covering human resources, marketing and technology as part of an expanding central services operation, which also helped to eliminate duplication in some areas. Andy Donaldson, who took over as group finance director on the retirement of Ian Hawkins in 2018, brought a more commercial approach to the finance department, expanding the use to technology to improve efficiency, and making it a priority for the finance function to add value to the business rather than focus on historical reporting. When Les Calder was appointed group technology director in 2018, his brief was to apply technology for the more efficient management of a more complex business. He increased the size of the technology team, bringing in people with more expertise, and established technology as a leading Group function. A properly structured helpdesk was created, and it became possible to implement more effective project management for tasks such as rolling out software across the Group. Applications were reviewed, ensuring the Group made the most of what it had, establishing more effective reporting and use of data. Additional functions were added, such as instant messaging and videoconferencing, making it easier to share information and ideas across companies. Group project teams became feasible, with the creation of inter-company and inter-departmental teams. Infrastructure was overhauled, internet connections were improved, capacity expanded and Group standards set out for the first time. As Scott Cairns observed, 'We're now a business beginning to understand and manipulate the data to grow and truly understand the business properly. We are becoming a data-driven enterprise.' For Mike Donaldson, 'continuing to strengthen our core skills and central functions is key for future acquisitions and the future growth of our business'.

In the same vein, new appointments reinforced the strategic role of the supervisory board. When Val Donaldson and Randolph Murray stepped down in 2015, they were replaced by George Morris, whose family business, Morris and Spottiswood, was a leading Scottish construction company, and Pamela Scott, the Global Operational Excellence Director for Diageo.

The supervisory board has been instrumental in making sure the operating board has focused on growth as well as day-to-day operations. While the relationship between the two boards works reasonably well, there is a need to cultivate better informal links between members of each board, which would help to create a better understanding of different points of view. In a bigger business, there is also an argument for expanding membership of the operating board to encompass better representation of central services.

While individual businesses retain their own cultures under their own managing directors, the latter appreciate how decisions need to be taken in the wider interests of the group, recognising the mutual interdependence of each group company. Among all managers there is a growing recognition that everyone benefits from the more co-ordinated promotion of a wider product range that comes from being part of a bigger enterprise.

Succession planning throughout the Group has become more critical. While the Group has continued to recruit talented individuals from outside the business, it has been crucial to develop the potential of those inside. For instance, Luke Roberts identified the need at Ilkeston to span the gap between the skills needed for team leaders and general managers. Creating assistant general manager posts, backed by associated training, has helped to cultivate and retain a pool of internal talent. This successful initiative has been extended throughout the whole Group, leading to a group-wide management training scheme. Senior staff have been assisted to enhance their skills, making them stronger managers, giving them the capacity to assume more responsibility as their businesses grow. Within MGM, for example, several employees have achieved the industry's diploma in merchanting, the prelude to a foundation degree in management. At the other end of the spectrum, the Group recruits apprentices every year, although finding enough people with the right skills for other vacancies is a challenge. 'What we've done well', said Luke Roberts, 'is develop our people: from top to bottom, people are our biggest asset.'

The transition of the business from one generation of the family to the next has been carefully planned.

It has been done so well, in fact, that, on the contrary, both Mike and Andy Donaldson have felt that their path through the business was opportunistic. While their father was deeply involved in this planning, the brothers were also helped by two other key figures. George Morris filled a vital role as an arm's-length mentor for the brothers, and Scott Cairns, as group managing director, made sure Mike and Andy were ready to assume leadership whenever Scott decided to step down. Neil, Mike and Andy all realised that the responsibility of being the first non-family managing director was a heavy one for Scott, who brought his own style to the role. Inevitably, he was driven by different considerations, and he admitted that he struggled with the concept of running a business owned by someone else: 'I thought of it as mine.' It was this conundrum that persuaded him to relinquish the role earlier than many people expected. But it was also this personal drive that brought about the Group's outstanding progress under his leadership. 'I have nothing but admiration for the job he has done', said Andy Donaldson.

The brothers rejected any idea that the Group should be slimmed down to make their future careers easier. They were eager for the challenge and determined to prove they were ready for it on merit. After managing Buckhaven for three years, Mike Donaldson moved to JDT for four years, where he helped to set up a waste reclamation operation. In 2015 he took up the role of commercial manager for MGM, becoming commercial director in 2017. Andy Donaldson took up a junior sales role with MGM in Edinburgh to learn more about MGM's customers and products before moving to JDT to work with Iain Torrance, tackling the challenges of the sites at

Brill and Chorley. Mike joined the supervisory board in 2014, and Andy did so in 2015. In 2018, as deputy chairman, Mike chaired the AGM for the first time in his father's absence. In the same year, Andy took over as group finance director. He enjoyed a close working relationship with Scott Cairns, who involved Andy closely in day-to-day management as well as in strategy, investment decisions and acquisition opportunities. It was an ideal preparation for taking over from Scott as chief executive in the spring of 2020. (Scott continued as a non-executive director to support Andy as he settled into his new post.) At the same time, Mike was preparing to take over as chairman on his father's retirement after the AGM that July.

What neither Andy nor Mike could have foreseen was the huge challenge to the business posed by the national lockdown declared in response to the emerging COVID-19 pandemic, which has struck the world. When the lockdown was announced on 23 March, a conference call with all the operating board directors was arranged for 9.30 pm. They took the decision to shut down the business immediately for the first time in its history, something neither of the world wars nor the Spanish flu pandemic of 1918–19

The huge challenge posed to the business by the national lockdown

had done. The following day, a small team of two to three people inspected each site to make sure they were all safe and secure. The question was how long would the business remain closed?

During the lockdown, the operating board, including Scott Cairns and Neil Donaldson, held daily conference calls, with a weekly call for the supervisory board. Cash management was critical. Initially it was assumed there would be no trading until the end of July; Andy Donaldson estimated the Group would run out of capital in ten weeks. Immediate steps were taken to conserve cash. Unnecessary cash expenditure was halted. All the cash from subsidiary accounts was transferred into the Group account and every advantage was taken of deferred tax payments and loan repayment holidays. Subsidiary accounts, left with a nil balance, were then used for receipts and payments, with money taken from customers paid out to suppliers. From the start, cash continued to come into the business as customers carried on paying their invoices, some of them settling early, allowing Donaldson's in turn to pay its suppliers, helping to keep cash flowing throughout the supply chain.

The company also took advantage of the government's furlough scheme, which subsidised employee wages. As well as providing financial relief, the scheme also obviated the need for the Group to lay people off and then re-employ them when business recovered. Almost all Donaldson's employees were placed on furlough, excepting a small team of some fifty senior people, including credit controllers and the head of finance, who had a key role in managing cash. Since DTE was still receiving enquiries, a handful of designers were also working remotely.

Staff were constantly enquiring when the business might reopen, partly because some rivals, self-defining themselves as essential businesses, were still operating; but Mike and Andy Donaldson, guided by the value the Group placed on people and family, insisted this would only happen when they could guarantee employees would be safe.

With the onset of the Covid pandemic in 2020, the company swiftly put in place measures to keep staff safe.

By comparison with the ease of shutting down the business, it was, the brothers agreed, much more difficult to reopen it. This was complicated by the differing advice offered by governments north and south of the border. As businesses reopened in England, they remained closed in Scotland. Messages from the Department for Business urged businesses to reopen – and there was continuing pressure from employees – yet the Scottish government was advising people to remain at home. All of this, however, was simply advice; none of it was legally binding, and it was down to the company to decide when it should reopen. An important consideration was having employees on both sides of the border returning to work at the same time.

The James Donaldson Group reopened on 4 May 2020. In preparation for this, small teams had been operating on every site the week before, making sure all the necessary steps had been taken to keep employees safe. There were staggered rotas for a return to work so that social distancing could be observed. Pods of people were devised, breaking up teams to minimise the possibility of everyone becoming infected. Signs were put in place, and desks were reorganised. There was a major communications campaign. Prior to reopening, Mike and Andy visited many of the company's sites to reassure themselves that they personally would be happy to return to work at each location. For sites they were unable to visit, they were given a remotely conducted tour by general managers using their mobile phones.

All except two sites reopened on 4 May. Rather than partially opening all DTE's operations to achieve the 70% capacity needed, two sites, Ashford and Enstone, remained closed, allowing every other location to operate at full output. In Scotland, where construction work had not restarted, manufacturing activities began with just a skeleton staff.

MGM's managing director, David Mansell, convinced Mike and Andy Donaldson that every one of its branches should open simultaneously. He was right: welcoming a flood of new retail customers investing in DIY after lockdown, MGM returned record results in July and August. This was not without challenges. As well as dealing with the inrush of many new individual customers, staff were faced with the administration of countless small orders, each one consuming just as much time as a much bigger single order for a trade customer. Products were difficult to source since many suppliers were still closed and their scarcity made them much more expensive. Nevertheless, the successful outcome reflected how well staff had risen to the task and how professionally the situation had been managed.

As a major supplier to MGM, JDT also boomed. The orders received by Elm Park on 4 May took two and a half days to process. As much decking was sold in a single day as in the entire month of May in the previous year. Crucially, managing the flurry of orders from MGM was achieved while simultaneously meeting the requirements of JDT's traditional trade customers.

The Group's other businesses resumed operations as construction activity revived. Obtaining raw material was not easy. Although Swedish timber mills had remained open during the UK's lockdown, they had sold timber usually destined for UK customers to the US. The resulting shortage pushed up prices significantly.

The newcomers to the Group, Rowan and Smith & Frater, also performed well, and their staff were relieved to be part of Donaldson's, doubting that the previous owners would have coped as well with the crisis.

The losses made by the Group in April and May were recouped in June and July, and by August the business had achieved a profit for the period. Nevertheless, the uncertainty created by the pandemic made the supervisory board understandably cautious about the future. Rejecting government loans available to them because of the inflexible conditions attached, the Group negotiated a further bank loan to provide comfort for the next 12 months.

For Mike and Andy Donaldson, the lasting impression of the crisis was the loyalty and commitment of every employee. 'It's been humbling to watch', said Andy. The brothers believed that the crisis helped them to make their own mark on the business much more quickly. They both recognised the importance of keeping in touch with every employee whether at work or on furlough. They introduced regular video presentations, initially weekly,

later fortnightly, on a variety of topics, each usually lasting no more than eight minutes or so, the exception being a rather longer one made by Andy on finance and the importance of husbanding cash. Videos were produced for each site on health and safety, allowing people to know what to expect before they returned to work, as well as a series of online sessions on matters such as hand washing, which each employee had to complete prior to returning. (These were picked up by trade bodies as exemplars for the industry.) The brothers also held question and answer sessions, responding to issues raised by employees. They promised that as soon as financially possible, the bonus due for the previous year's results would be honoured. All this was very well received. Speaking to people directly prevented miscommunication and misunderstanding.

For the Donaldson family, their direct and visible involvement as senior managers and shareholders is a sign of the family's continuing commitment to the business and its employees. While the family holds three quarters of the shares, they believe the growth of the business will offer the scope to increase the proportion of shares held by employees, who must sell them back to the company when they leave. George Donaldson, who died in 2016 at the age of ninety,

The crisis 'allowed us to grab the business by the scruff of the neck'

always believed that this would strengthen the bonds between employee and business. As Scott Cairns reflected, share ownership gives the feeling that 'you are part of something bigger than yourself'. This, he believed, had been a critical factor in the cohesion, drive and performance of the senior management team.

Unlike external shareholders, however, the family can take a much longer view about the future of the business; they are, Neil Donaldson stresses, stewards of the business for generations to come. His father, George, had no doubt that the business largely owed its resilience to the advantages of being a private family company. 'Properly run,' he said, 'it strengthens links between members of the family, it enables the enterprise

The Group sees the employee share-ownership scheme (currently there are some fifty employee shareholders) and other incentives as crucial for rewarding achievement. So too is developing the skills of talented individuals and creating new opportunities for them. Long service remains a tradition within the Group – the two most recent of the forty-six employees to achieve more than twenty years' service were James Moonie and Willie Gardiner, both from MGM, who celebrated twenty-five years with Donaldson's in the summer of 2020. In 2015, Andrew Waddell recorded fifty-five years of service with the Group.

The next generation around the handsome inlaid board table at the company's head office in Glenrothes.

to concentrate on long-term goals rather than market pressures, it tends to strengthen relationships between the family and those whose careers are built on it.'

For the family, there was a need to create a vehicle to allow immediate family members to discuss matters pertinent to their interests but outside the scope of the supervisory board. It would also permit the involvement of members of the immediate family who were not directors. The Family Forum is a relatively recent creation but it allows the family, including Neil's wife, Val, and their daughter, Jennifer, to contribute. It also involves the non-executive members of the supervisory board.

The success of the business rests on everyone working within it

Three generations of the Donaldson family gathered to celebrate the unveiling of Maggie Milne's portrait of George Donaldson at Glenrothes on 9 October 2018.

The Donaldson Leadership Academy

As the business approached its 150th anniversary, Neil Donaldson wanted to mark the occasion in a lasting and constructive way in sympathy with the Donaldson ethos. The result was the Donaldson Leadership Academy, a registered charity, with family members Val, Michael, Andrew and Jennifer Donaldson as trustees. It came about through Neil's friendship with Norman Drummond, well known for his commitment to public service in Scotland and his work in leadership development. In 1997 he founded Columba 1400, the first purpose-built community and international leadership centre in the UK. Located on the Isle of Skye, Columba 1400 works with young people from disadvantaged backgrounds, helping to release their potential as leaders and contributors within their own communities.

This struck a chord with Neil Donaldson. The company invested £150,000, or £1,000 for every year since the foundation of the business, in the Donaldson Leadership Academy. The income from this investment allowed the charity to fund the participation of sixteen young people every year on a course at Columba 1400. The participants were drawn from the company's home territory in Fife, which has a record as one of the most deprived areas in Scotland. The local education department put the company in touch with two local schools, Buckhaven High School and Kirkland High School, which later merged to become Levenmouth Academy in 2016. Each course, lasting six days, is a daunting but revelatory experience for those taking part. For Neil and Val Donaldson, witnessing the transformation when they attended one course was 'unbelievably emotional'. During the 150th anniversary year, the company invited suppliers and others to contribute towards funding to match the company's investment in the Academy, which allowed twice as many young people to take advantage of this life-changing opportunity.

Donaldson Leadership Academy students from Levenmouth Academy celebrating their success.

In 2021, more than 160 years after James Donaldson founded his business, the company is still sawing softwood, shown here at Elm Park.

There are many reasons for the successful longevity of James Donaldson & Sons. Over the generations, the family has worked well together, with little strife, partly by accepting that differing aptitudes are complementary and not conflicting. The family has recognised that the success of the business rests on everyone working within it, which has fostered long service, loyalty and trust. In recent times, the family has also recognised the value talented outsiders can bring to the business, not just through non-executive appointments to the board, but also in the external recruitment of senior managers. There has been a willingness to accept the need for change to take the business forward, accompanied, however, by a conservative approach to finance, stemming from long experience of a volatile industry. Long-term customer relationships have always been prized. Underpinning all this is an ambition to remain independent, with each successive generation seeing itself as stewards of the business built up by their predecessors. For George Donaldson, speaking in 2010, 'this belief in the responsibility to build on our inheritance, shared by the family, passed on now to

Above: The digital AGM held during the Covid pandemic: (top row) Val Donaldson, Bill Donaldson and Arlene Cairns; (middle row) Sarah Donaldson, David Sadler and Colin Rutherford; (bottom row) Jim Savage, Neil Donaldson and Anya Mayor.

Opposite: Andy and Mike Donaldson.

the sixth generation, is the unique distinguishing mark of our business'. All this marks out James Donaldson & Sons as one of the few modern-day success stories of an industry that has changed radically since the business was founded. Under the leadership of Mike and Andy Donaldson, emulating their great-grandfather Victor and great-great-uncle Reg, James Donaldson & Sons is at an exciting point in its history. The brothers are already asking fundamental questions about the Group's further evolution, ambitious to carry on its growth and secure its future. They recognise that Donaldson's must continue to adapt; as Andy said, 'if we want to be here for the next generation, we need to change with it'.

Acknowledgements

Many people contributed towards the preparation of the two previous editions as well as this completely new and updated edition marking the retirement of Neil Donaldson and the appointment of Mike Donaldson as chairman and Andy Donaldson as chief executive officer. Those who kindly contributed to this and previous editions include Bill Allan, Scott Cairns, Les Calder, Douglas Campsie, Andy Donaldson, Bill Donaldson, Colin Donaldson, Jean Donaldson, George Donaldson, Mike Donaldson, Neil Donaldson, Jonathan Fellingham, Ian Hawkins, Callum Henderson, Ian Johnston, Randolph Murray, Harry Robb, Luke Roberts, Alan Sinclair, Iain Torrance, Andy Waddell and George Watson. I would also like to thank Deborah Palmer for her help over many years. Any errors which remain may be attributed to the author.

Nigel Watson

Donaldson Timeline

Date	Event
1860	James Donaldson begins business in Tayport on 28 September
1863	George Donaldson senior establishes timber business in South Alloa
1870	James Donaldson junior joins the firm
1875	George Donaldson senior absconds from justice to the United States
1876	James Donaldson junior becomes a partner
1878	Tay Bridge built
1887	R G E Wemyss builds new dock at Methil
1888	George Donaldson junior becomes a partner
1889	James Donaldson & Sons acquires Leven timber business
1892	Formation of Timber Trade Federation
1910	Jubilee auction and dinner held on 28 September
1914	Victor Donaldson joins the firm but soon leaves on active service
1917	Timber Control established
1918	Government timber stocks disposed of through Associated Importers
1919	James Donaldson & Sons Ltd formed: William Reid appointed first non-family director
1921	Reg Donaldson joins the company
1923	Victor Donaldson appointed director
1927	Reg Donaldson appointed director
1932	Tayport mill modernised
1936	George Donaldson retires as managing director in favour of his sons
1936	Victor Donaldson becomes president of the Scottish Timber Merchants' & Sawmillers' Association

Date	Event
1937	Victor Donaldson becomes chairman
1938	J D Barron appointed director
1940	Victor Donaldson appointed Area Officer for Timber Control
1945	Government stocks of timber disposed of through National Softwood Brokers
1948	George Donaldson joins the company
1952	Last horse sold at Tayport
1953	George Donaldson appointed director
1953	Last state controls over timber industry abolished
1954	Dredging agreement reached for Tayport harbour
1955	Elm Park yard acquired
1956	Colin Donaldson joins the company
1957	J D Barron retires
1957	James Donaldson & Sons Ltd becomes first Scottish timber company to acquire a forklift truck
1959	Rail tracks at Tayport and Wemyss yard taken up
1962	Tayport Harbour acquired
1964	Colin Donaldson appointed director
1964	Five-day working week introduced
1969	Retirement of Victor Donaldson from executive duties
1969	George Donaldson appointed managing director
1970	Robert Walker appointed director
1971	George Donaldson becomes chairman
1971	Leven yard badly damaged by fire
1973	New offices opened in Riverside Place
1975	George Donaldson becomes president of the Scottish Timber Merchants' & Sawmillers' Association
1975	Neil Donaldson joins company
1976	New mill at Elm Park opened
1976	Ron Dickson, Bob Cumming & Archie Honeyman appointed directors
1977	Colin Donaldson leaves company to train as minister
1978	Home Improvement Centre opens

Date	Event
1978	Roof truss manufacturing starts under George Watson
1979	Alan Sinclair appointed director
1980	George Donaldson becomes chairman of TRADA
1983	J & A Hutton Ltd acquired
1984	Bob Cumming retires
1985	Ron Dickson retires
1985	George R Donaldson and Robin Young appointed first non-executive directors
1985	George Donaldson becomes president of the Timber Trade Federation
1985	Neil Donaldson takes over as managing director
1986	Donaldson Timber Engineering Ltd formed and Muiredge factory acquired
1990	Tayport depot closes
1992	Death of Archie Honeyman
1992	Cramlington factory established
1995	Donaldson Timber Engineering (Midlands) Ltd formed
1996	Scott Cairns joins company
1997	Wemyss yard sold for redevelopment as supermarket
1997	Firstbase joint venture begins
1998	James Donaldson Timber Ltd formed
1999	Firstbase stake sold
2000	George Donaldson awarded CBE
2000	Neil Donaldson becomes TRADA chairman
2000	Ashford factory established
2000	Website launched
2001	Andover factory established
2001	George Donaldson retires as chairman and is appointed honorary president
2001	Neil Donaldson becomes chairman
2001	50% stake taken in Parker Kislingbury
2001	Ian Hawkins appointed financial director
2001	50% stake taken in MGM

Date	Event
2003	DTE Ireland established
2004	Ipswich factory established
2004	Investment portfolio placed under the management of Adam & Co
2005	Michael Donaldson joins the business
2005	MGM becomes wholly owned part of the group
2006	Neil Donaldson becomes president of the Timber Trade Federation
2006	Iain Torrance is appointed Managing Director, JDT
2006	Scott Cairns becomes Managing Director, MGM
2006	Parker Kislingbury becomes wholly owned part of the group
2006	Ilkeston sawmill closes
2008	Alfred Hulme, Chorley, acquired
2008	Donaldson Leadership Academy established
2009	Alan Sinclair retires from executive responsibilities
2010	Andrew Donaldson joins the business
2010	James Donaldson Group celebrates its 150th anniversary
2011	Scott Cairns appointed group managing director
2012	Neil Donaldson is the first recipient of the Timber Trade Federation's Lifetime Achievement Award
2012	James Donaldson Insulation Ltd formed
2015	Closure of Parker Kislingbury, Brill
2016	Death of George Donaldson
2016	New head office completed and occupied in Glenrothes
2016	Nu Style acquired
2018	Cambridge Roof Truss Ltd acquired
2018	Mike Donaldson becomes deputy chairman; Andy Donaldson becomes group finance director
2020	Acquisition of Rowan Manufacturing Ltd and Smith & Frater Ltd
2020	Mike Donaldson succeeds Neil Donaldson as chairman
2020	Andy Donaldson succeeds Scott Cairns as group managing director

Financial Statistics

Date	Turnover £	Operating Profits £	Shareholders' Funds £
1919–20	212,883	13,982	106,968
1920–21	206,854	-8,835	80,000
1921–22	139,211	64,89	93,021
1922–23	136,665	5,857	99,452
1923–24	159,057	3,941	97,422
1924–25	155,966	3,126	93,753
1925–26	158,911	-939	81,649
1926–27	147,823	4,612	91,948
1927–28	148,848	1,126	93,217
1928–29	138,276	79	84,382
1929–30	127,790	217	85,488
1930–31	103,435	-6,578	71,924
1931–32	104,829	-2,244	73,077
1932–33	116,772,	278	75,728
1933–34	143,765	-405	83,903
1934–35	150,931	-4,895	74,459
1935–36	156,844	2,281	83,301
1936–37	203,929	5,078	101,887
1937–38	211,575	-1,336	10,1843
1938–39	167,507	182	99,183
1939–40	192,012	20,430	135,791
1940–41	139,877	11,776	118,309
1941–42	138,664	6,840	130,730
1942–43	129,127	5,246	128,611
1943–44	146,320	3,943	127,755
1944–45	201,370	10,315	135,824
1945–46	192,618	8,366	126,357
1946–47	269,806	21,216	137,670

Date	Turnover £	Operating Profits £	Shareholders' Funds £
1947–48	381,690	21,250	149,158
1948–49	448,556	33,659	171,005
1949–50	401,578	22112	18,2590
1950–51	418,776	25,272	195,047
1951–52	600,495	11267	197,273
1952–53	641,325	33,535	217,845
1953–54	594,550	24,294	230,963
1954–55	621,837	21,758	241,058
1955–56	607,856	17,051	238,181
1956–57	635,882	13,414	246,447
1957–58	612,595	10592	243,424
1958–59	575,596	6,716	235,045
1959–60	667,761	26,798	255,698
1960–61	697,639	18,679	260,067
1961–62	724,679	13,194	257,174
1962–63	666,374	8,150	253,118
1963–64	785,850	17,711	267,833
1964–65	878,691	19,462	292,087
1965–66	930,369	7,397	300249
1966–67	997,950	7,212	300,412
1967–68	1,095,226	2,5107	330,657
1968–69	1,072,034	16,520	360,540
1969–70	1,092,061	19,815	369,190
1970–71	1,130,115	20,489	376,945
1971–72	1,256,250	43,032	412,510
1972–73	1,507,066	78,905	518,735
1973–74	1,764,623	264,450	720 807
1974–75	3,056,322	107,236	779 905
1975–76	3,308,019	205,456	898 446
1976–77	3,992,426	214,659	1,088,033
1977–78	4,017,973		1,124,837
1978–79	4,407,829		1,336,031
1979–80	5,567,880		1,419,300
1980–81	5,948,620		1,656,561
1981–82	6,366,840	-1,401	1,436,911
1982–83	7,042,565	284,593	1,484,027

Date	Turnover £	Operating Profits £	Shareholders' Funds £
1983–84	7,893,132		1,731,629
1984–85	8,918,685	385,923	1,758,119
1985–86	10,500,977	427,257	1,698,232
1986–87	11,311,931	60,027	1,624,520
1987–88	13,629,200	368,945	1,887,263
1988–89	17,412,820	595,885	2,283,442
1989–90	21,116,273	861,917	2,737,282
1990–91	22,199,715	324,233	3,538,887
1991–92	20,790,150	-181,695	3,355,819
1992–93	21,533,293		3,091,779
1993–94	23,726,670	366,279	3,091,779
1994–95	27,105,495	1,186,985	3,400,741
1995–96	28,255,140	-211,474	4,470,315
1996–97*	30,887	739	4,535
1997–98	28,348	698	5,417
1998–99	27,889	1,163	5,969
1999–2000	35,995	1,298	7,430
2000–01	35,913	1,468	8,052
2001–02	37,531	1,632	8,820
2002–03	41,647	1,696	9,664
2003–04	44,211	1,861	10,665
2004–05	46,287	1,819	10,079
2005–06	66,926	2,112	10,939
2006–07	75,485	3,558	13,694
2007–08	97,415	3,596	15,954
2008–09	78,095	874	15,423
2009–10	80,727	887	14,721
2010–11	97,350	2,110	16,544
2011–12	105,345	2,124	17,208
2012–13	105,379	2,526	17,982
2013–14	117,177	2,831	18,867
2014–15	132,733	4,798	21,138
2015–16	127,051	6,123	26,617
2016–17	136,553	7,526	29,598
2017–18	153,592	7,701	33,778
2018–19	182,028	8,605	39,520

* Figures hereafter in £000s

Index